The

Art

of

Non-war

The Art
of
Non-war

Kim Michaels

More to Life Publishing

The Art of Non-war
by Kim Michaels.
Copyright © 2007 by Kim Michaels and
More to Life Publishing.

All rights reserved.

No part of this book may be reproduced, translated or
transmitted by any means except by written permission
from the publisher. A reviewer may quote brief passages
in a review.

Library of Congress control number: 2007907901.

ISBN-10: 0-9766971-9-X.

ISBN-13: 978-0-9766971-9-0.

Printed in the United States of America.

Other books by Kim Michaels:

I Love Jesus, I Hate Christianity

The Least You Should Know About Life

Beyond Religious Conflict

I Am a Thinking Christian

The Inner Path of Light

Table of Contents

Introduction **7**

Chapter 1. Preparing for Non-war **10**

Chapter 2. Waging Non-war **34**

Chapter 3. Non-attack by Incomparable Stratagem **43**

Chapter 4. Non-dual Tactical Dispositions **62**

Chapter 5. Energy from the Infinite **84**

Chapter 6. Beyond Strong and Weak Points **95**

Chapter 7. Non-dualistic Maneuvering **118**

Chapter 8. Non-dual Variation in Tactics **128**

Chapter 9. The Warriors of Peace on the March **136**

Chapter 10. Knowing Physical and Non-physical Terrain **150**

Chapter 11. Non-dual Situations **180**

Chapter 12. The Use of Spiritual Fire **201**

Chapter 13. Non-dualistic Foreknowledge **206**

Chapter 14. Knowing Duality and Non-duality **208**

Introduction

In a previous age, a teacher of duality, known as Sun Tzu, became the instrument for releasing a manuscript about the art of war. It is a cosmic law that whenever a dualistic teaching is released, there must be the release of a non-dualistic teaching in order to give people a choice between duality and non-duality.

In that previous age, a teaching was released to give people a choice between duality and non-duality, between death and Life. Yet because the people of that age were blinded by selfish pursuits, they paid little attention—preferring instead to use the dualistic teaching to secure some temporary advantage.

The original non-dualistic teaching was ignored, neglected, forgotten and eventually lost. Yet the dualistic teaching was preserved, and it gave many selfish people a justification for taking their selfish pursuits into greater depths of insensitivity to life.

In the modern age, the dualistic teaching has been revived, partly to be used in the field of business. And again, many people have used it as a justification for entrapping themselves even more firmly in the illusion that a selfish act can lead to a lasting advantage. Thus, cosmic law requires that a non-dualistic teaching be released in order to – once again – give people a real choice between death and Life. That non-dualistic teaching is contained in this book.

The original manuscript of the dualistic teacher has survived, but the teacher himself has long since perished, destroyed by his own selfish pursuits. The original manuscript of the non-dualistic teacher was lost, but the teacher survived, for in oneness with the Infinite there is no death. Thus, the same teacher has released this new manuscript, keeping largely true to the original but with certain updates to make it more useful to people in the present age.

It is the hope that this release will gain more widespread acceptance and use than the original. For in the modern age, the weapons of war are so powerful that even Sun Tzu would have revised his manuscript, had he known their destructive power. Naturally, as the destructive power of weapons is increased, the potential cost of war goes up, and thus even a person blinded by duality can see the necessity of reconsidering armed conflict.

It is the hope that sufficient numbers of people will see the value of taking an even higher approach by rising above the consciousness that creates war, namely the dualistic mind. For only if enough people are willing to reach beyond duality, can there be a release of the wisdom and energy that will consume the engines of war and bring true and lasting peace.

This book is a gift to those who know in their hearts that the time is long past when war and the consciousness of war should have been purged from the Earth. Therefore, they are willing to make an extraordinary effort to make themselves the open doors for the River of Life. They are willing to serve in clearing the stream of humankind's consciousness, until all see that they do have a choice between their current state of spiritual death and the state of incomparable Life.

May the practitioners of the art of non-war come forward in time to prevent the practitioners of the art of war from creating a momentum that cannot be stopped, and thus releases the destructive power that has been accumulated by those who still believe in the ancient lie that the ends can justify the means.

May the practitioners of non-war bring the light that can illumine the minds of all to the fact that one cannot stop war by seeking to destroy the enemy, but only by awakening the enemy to the reality of Life. Yet in order to awaken another, one must first remove the consciousness of war from one's own mind.

This teaching is a gift to those who have realized the timeless truth that in order to change the world, one must begin by changing oneself.

Chapter 1.
Preparing for Non-war

The dualistic mind says:

The art of war is of vital importance to the State. It is a matter of life and death, a road either to safety or to ruin. Hence it is a subject of inquiry which must be studied thoroughly.

The non-dualistic mind says:

War is indeed a matter of vital importance, both for the individual, for the state and for humanity. Thus, it is vital that war be studied thoroughly. Yet a topic can be studied thoroughly only through the non-dualistic mind.

When approached through the filter of the dualistic mind, war is not a matter of life or death. For there is no life in war; only death.

When approached through the filter of the dualistic mind, war is not the road to safety or ruin. For there is no safety in war; only ruin.

Only the dualistic mind sees war as an option, as a means to achieve any desirable end.

Only the dualistic mind can believe in the illusion that taking from others through force can secure permanent gain for oneself.

Only the dualistic mind can believe in the illusion that inflicting death upon others can secure life for oneself.

Only the dualistic mind can believe in the illusion that inflicting ruin upon others can lead to one's own safety.

Only the dualistic mind can believe that the end can justify the means, so that the end of securing one's own wealth or safety can justify the means of taking by force and killing others.

The reason is that there is no life in the dualistic mind; only death. Thus, the dualistic mind does not see infinite truth; only a finite illusion of its own making.

***

A thorough study of war should lead to an understanding of the cause of war. Then what is the real cause of war?

It is the illusion of separation from the Infinite!

The dualistic mind was born from this illusion, and it can never see the unreality of this illusion. Thus, anything done by the dualistic mind can only reinforce the illusion of separation.

Once a mind believes in the illusion of separation from the Infinite, it inevitably follows that the mind believes in the illusion of lack. For there is no lack in the Infinite. Thus, only when the mind thinks it is separated from the Infinite, can it believe in the illusion of lack.

Only when the mind believes in the illusion of lack, can it believe that there can be gain in taking from others through force—rather than seeking what one desires directly from the Infinite.

12

Thus, the true cause of war is the illusion of lack, which leads to the illusion of gain through force.

The dualistic mind precipitates threats to its survival by projecting its own duality into the cosmic mirror. It does not see that its own internal duality is what leads to conflict and thus precipitates its own enemies.

Once the dualistic mind has precipitated an enemy, it believes that only by destroying the enemy can it secure its own survival. Yet the dualistic mind fails to see that the use of force will only precipitate another enemy. For as long as there is duality, there must be opposing forces.

The dualistic mind might win a temporary victory over an outer enemy, and thus seemingly find safety. Yet any use of force will inevitably create another enemy, and in time it will grow to become a threat to one's survival.

Ultimate survival can be attained only by transcending the dualistic mind so one no longer precipitates enemies. This self-transcendence to a state of ultimate freedom is the highest outcome of a thorough study of war.

***

The greatest of all illusions is the illusion of separation from the Infinite. This primary illusion leads to the illusion of lack. Yet the illusion of lack can take on many disguises, and many of them can lead to war.

There are two chief illusions that lead to war.

One is the illusion that the Earth is a world with a limited amount of resources. This causes the dualistic mind to believe in the further illusion that there is a direct proportion between the amount of material resources available and the amount of abundance that can be created.

The dualistic mind now believes that in order to obtain more abundance, one must take from someone else. This causes people to enter an endless struggle of competition for a greater slice of what is perceived to be a finite pie of abundance.

The non-dualistic mind sees that there is far greater abundance in the world today than a thousand years ago. It also sees that the Earth is not larger and does not have more land or resources than a thousand years ago.

The non-dualistic mind sees that the greater amount of abundance is possible only because some people have learned to draw wisdom and energy directly from the Infinite, using it to precipitate more wealth and thereby enlarge the finite pie.

The non-dualistic mind sees that because all things in the world of form are made of energy from the infinite world of formlessness, there is no limit to the amount of abundance that can be precipitated. Thus, it is auspicious to focus one's efforts on learning how to precipitate wealth directly from the Infinite, instead of entering the struggle for a greater slice of a finite amount.

The non-dualistic mind sees that if all people learned how to draw upon the Infinite, there would be no more need for war over wealth, for no one would need to take anything from anyone else. Thus, the reason why there is still war in the world is that so many people are ignorant of the Infinite and the potential to precipitate abundance from this incomparable and inexhaustible source.

The non-dualistic mind sees that ignorance is the cause of war. The cause of ignorance is the illusion of separation. Thus, in order to learn how to draw abundance from the

14

Infinite, one must be willing to overcome one's sense of separation from the Infinite. This then points to a viable path that can lead—not to victory in war but to victory over war.

**

The second major cause of war is conflict over ideas.

The dualistic mind is blinded by the illusion of separation and cannot perceive the Infinite. Thus, it believes in the illusion that the living truth can be confined to a static framework – a theory, philosophy or belief system – in the finite world.

The dualistic mind fails to see that when the infinite truth becomes clothed in a finite framework, every idea must have an opposite idea. The dualistic mind fails to see that while an idea expressed in the finite world might contain elements of truth, the finite expression of truth is not the same as the incomparable truth of the Infinite. An expression of truth is not the same as the Spirit of Truth.

The dualistic mind now believes that its preferred idea is true in an ultimate sense and that the idea that opposes it is false in an ultimate sense. Thus, the dualistic mind believes it is justified in using force to destroy the opposing idea and that this will secure the survival of its preferred idea.

Behind these illusions is – again – the illusion of lack. The dualistic mind believes that there are limits for how truth can be expressed, and it has elevated one particular expression of truth as an absolute truth that could never be transcended. This "absolute" truth has defined limits for what people can understand about the world.

The non-dualistic mind sees that humanity has a far greater understand of the world today than a thousand years ago. Yet the world is not larger than it was in the past. So the greater understanding is possible only because some people have learned to draw upon the incomparable and inexhaustible wisdom of the Infinite. They have been willing to transcend a finite expression of truth in order to attain a greater understanding of the Infinite than was expressed in their old thought system.

The non-dualistic mind knows that the reason why there is greater understanding in the world today is that some people have engaged in an ongoing quest to have their finite understanding and experience of truth come ever closer to the Infinite. This empowers them to precipitate a life that is abundant both materially and spiritually.

The non-dualistic mind sees that if all people learned how to draw understanding directly from the Infinite, there would be no more need for war over ideas, for no one would need to cling to a finite expression of truth as being absolute. They would instead focus on the quest of receiving a progressive revelation of wisdom directly from the Infinite.

The reason why there is still war in the world is that so many people are ignorant of the Infinite and the potential to draw understanding from it.

The non-dualistic mind sees that ignorance is the cause of war. The cause of ignorance is the illusion of separation. Thus, in order to learn how to draw understanding from the Infinite, one must be willing to overcome one's sense of separation from the Infinite. This then points to a viable path that can lead—not to victory in war but to victory over war.

***

The non-dualistic mind sees that human beings are designed with a survival instinct. This instinct has both an individual, a collective and an overall aspect.

On the individual level, if one person sees another person as a threat to his or her survival, many people will kill another human being in order to survive. On the collective level, if the members of one group of people see another group as a threat to the survival of the group, they will kill all members of the competing group in order to survive.

On the overall level, all human beings are designed to work for the survival of the human race. Thus, the need to secure the survival of the whole will temper the willingness to kill individuals and groups.

Killing is possible only when the concern for individual and group survival seems to override the concern for survival of the whole. It now seems as if the survival of the whole necessitates the killing of an individual or all members of a group, for they have been designated as threats to the whole.

Yet the sense that an individual or group is a threat to the whole springs from the illusion of lack. The illusion of lack gives rise to the belief that individual and group survival is linked to the preservation of finite resources or finite expressions of truth. Thus, a threat to one's wealth or idea is seen as a threat to the survival of an individual, a group or perhaps even humanity as a whole.

This gives rise to the illusion that killing is necessary and justified in order to secure the survival of oneself, one's group or the entire human race. Yet only the dualistic mind can believe that killing can secure life.

The dualistic mind believes this because it is separated from the Infinite and thus cannot see that the *only* source of true life and true abundance is the Infinite. The dualistic mind cannot see that by refusing to kill over finite resources, one will attain an incomparable reward from the Infinite—a reward that is more valuable than finite ideas, finite resources or even one's finite life.

The dualistic mind will always seek to hold on to what it thinks it possesses in the finite world, for it cannot see that in the finite world nothing is permanent and thus nothing can be owned. Therefore, the dualistic mind does not see that in seeking to save its finite life, it is separating itself even more from the incomparable life that comes only through union with the Infinite.

The dualistic mind says:

The art of war, then, is governed by five constant factors, to be taken into account in one's deliberations.

The non-dualistic mind says:

War is not an art, for war is fighting a finite battle with a finite enemy. True art is a finite expression that connects people to the Infinite reality beyond the expression.

War is not governed by five constant factors, for there is nothing constant in the finite world, nor in the dualistic mind. To find truly constant factors for one's deliberations, one must access the Infinite.

The dualistic mind says:

The five constant factors are: (1) The Moral Law; (2) Heaven; (3) Earth; (4) The Commander; (5) Method and discipline.

The Moral Law causes the people to be in complete accord with their ruler, so that they will follow him regardless of their lives, undismayed by any danger.

The non-dualistic mind says:

Only the dualistic mind can operate with a view of humanity that makes some people superior to others; that makes some people rulers and others followers. This view is based on the illusion of separation, which makes it impossible to see that all humans came from the same source, namely the Infinite.

In the Infinite there is no separation and thus no space for comparisons that can make one infinite being superior to another. For how can there be divisions in infinity, and how can there be comparisons without divisions?

Only the dualistic mind can believe that moral law means that people recognize a ruler in the finite world and vow to follow that ruler blindly, even if it means losing their lives.

The non-dualistic mind sees that this is not moral law, but the height of immorality.

The non-dualistic mind sees that humans have no obligation to put a ruler in the finite world before the one true ruler, namely the Infinite.

When humans recognize the Infinite as the true ruler – and as the only source of moral law – they will never blindly follow a leader in the finite world.

Surely, people will realize that there are positions of leadership and that some people must fill these positions. Yet the people will always evaluate whether a person in a leadership position is in alignment with the Infinite and whether the leader's rule and commands are based on true moral law.

If the people see that a person in a leadership position is out of alignment with the Infinite and instead worships a finite expression as the source of moral law, then the people are free to refuse to follow such a leader. Certainly, they are free to preserve their lives by refusing to fight a war for an immoral leader.

True moral law causes people to be in complete accord with their true leader, namely the Infinite in the kingdom within them. Only if a finite ruler is also in complete accord with the Infinite, should people follow that leader.

If the leader is out of accord with the incomparable moral law, non-violent civil disobedience becomes the highest moral responsibility for the people.

The dualistic mind says:

Heaven signifies night and day, cold and heat, times and seasons.

Earth comprises distances, great and small; danger and security; open ground and narrow passes; the chances of life and death.

The non-dualistic mind says:

Only the dualistic mind can see Heaven in terms of finite conditions. Surely, "Heaven" is a symbol for the Infinite in which there can be no conditions.

Only the dualistic mind can see Earth in terms of finite conditions. Surely, Earth is only a finite clothing that the Infinite is wearing temporarily, for without the Infinite was not any thing made that was made. The non-dualistic mind sees beyond appearances to the hidden cause behind the effects that are visible to the senses.

Once the mind sees that the cause behind all appearances is the Infinite, it cannot be fooled by the dualistic illusion that finite appearances are real, permanent or unavoidable. Thus, the mind cannot be fooled into believing that finite conditions can turn other people into enemies and that destroying them can secure one's permanent gain or survival.

For how can permanency be attained by fighting impermanent appearances? Surely, permanency can be found only by looking beyond all finite conditions and reuniting with the Infinite.

The dualistic mind says:

The Commander stands for the virtues of wisdom, sincerity, benevolence, courage and strictness.

The non-dualistic mind says:

True wisdom is to see the Infinite as the first cause behind all finite appearances.

The true virtue of wisdom is to always put the Infinite before any finite conditions, thus never confusing cause and effect, never fighting appearances but basing one's life on the reality that separation is an illusion.

True sincerity comes from seeking union with the Infinite before any finite goals. True benevolence comes from seeing all other people as expressions of the Infinite that one has seen in oneself. True courage comes from pursuing the incomparable cause of the Infinite before any finite causes. True strictness comes from never allowing the illusions and energies of duality to enter one's mind.

Thus, people have no obligation to follow a commander who expresses finite virtues but has not discovered true wisdom and thus does not have true virtue.

The dualistic mind says:

By method and discipline are to be understood the marshaling of the army in its proper subdivisions, the graduations of rank among the officers, the maintenance of roads by which supplies may reach the army, and the control of military expenditure.

The non-dualistic mind says:

Once the mind has become engaged in the considerations for how to organize and supply an army, the battle is already lost.

True method means the study of how to avoid a finite war, so that one's attention and energy is not consumed by fighting a battle against appearances.

Instead, one's attention and energy is free to focus on learning how to draw abundance and understanding from the Infinite. Thereby, one can open the way for the precipitation of greater wealth, whereby all can be enriched without having to take from others.

One can open the way for bringing forth greater wisdom, whereby all can be enlightened and see beyond the need to fight the illusory battle of opposing ideas.

The dualistic mind says:

These five heads should be familiar to every general: he who knows them will be victorious; he who knows them not will fail.

The non-dualistic mind says:

Those who have true wisdom know that all generals are destined to fail. For a general is a leader in a finite army that is designed to fight another finite army in a dualistic battle based on appearances.

In a dualistic battle, there must be two opposing sides. In the short run, one side might appear to have won a victory. Yet in the long run, all those who engage in the dualistic struggle will fail.

For how can there be permanent victory in the finite world of appearances? How can victory be achieved by fighting a finite enemy, when the concept of enemies can only be based on appearances?

Those who engage in a battle based on appearances will ultimately fail, for they are seeking victory by reinforcing the illusion of separation. True victory, incomparable victory, can be attained only by reuniting with the Infinite.

When one unites oneself with the Infinite, one sees that all finite forms have the Infinite as their ultimate source. Thus, there can be no opposing sides, meaning that there can be no enemies. When there are no opposing sides, the concept of fighting a battle to defeat the enemy becomes meaningless.

People can then use true wisdom to overcome the illusion of separation. Thereby, they place themselves on the way that leads to incomparable victory, a victory in which all people win, for all grow in abundance and understanding.

The dualistic mind says:

Therefore, in your deliberations, when seeking to determine the military conditions, let them be made on the basis of a comparison.

The non-dualistic mind says:

Basing one's deliberations on a comparison of the appearances and conditions in the finite world can lead only to ruin and death. To have true deliberations, one must begin with a clear recognition of reality. Reality is that beyond finite appearances is the Infinite. The Infinite is the source of all finite forms, thus it is the source of all self-aware beings.

When you know that you are an expression of the Infinite, you will know that all other people are also expressions of the Infinite. Thus, the concept of conflict between you and others cannot come from the Infinite. It can be only a finite appearance, an illusion that springs from the mind of duality.

Engaging in the illusion of having to fight an enemy only takes you further away from union with the Infinite. And since the Infinite is the true source of abundance and wisdom, seeking to fight a finite war can never lead to true gain or survival.

True abundance and ongoing life can be found only in going beyond all finite appearances and exercising one's potential to unite with one's source. Thereby, the finite being becomes one with its infinite source—and thus sees its oneness with all other beings who came from that source.

The dualistic mind says:

(1) Which of the two sovereigns is imbued with the Moral law?

The non-dualistic mind says:

This is one of the most dangerous and subtle illusions of all.

The dualistic mind springs from separation from the Infinite. When this separation occurs, there is no longer oneness, which means that you have the simultaneous creation of two sides. These sides can only be opposites, and thus they are locked in an ongoing battle in which each side is seeking to annihilate the other side.

The very foundation for war is the creation of an illusion that makes it seem like there are two opposing sides and that there can be only conflict between them. This gives rise to the further illusion that one side can gain from conquering and destroying the other. Which gives rise to the further illusion that wealth and survival can be attained by conquering or destroying the enemy.

Yet by partaking in the illusion of separation, one has only reinforced one's separation from the Infinite and thus reinforced the wall – a wall that exists only in one's own mind and heart – that separates one from the incomparable abundance of the Infinite.

To people blinded by the dualistic mind, the conflict between the two sides seems real, and it seems like they truly are enemies. This then gives rise to the illusion that fuels all war, namely that one side is right in an absolute sense and that one side is wrong in an absolute sense.

The dualistic mind believes that one side has the moral law and that the other does not.

The non-dualistic mind sees that whenever there is conflict between two sides, none of them can have the moral law, for both are separated from the Infinite.

Thus, it is an illusion that one side has the moral law. Why is this an illusion? Because when one believes that one side has the moral law, then one also believes that it is morally right for that side to kill its enemy.

Yet has not the message from the Infinite consistently been the same, though it has been expressed in different forms? And has that message not always been, "Thou shalt not kill!"

The Infinite is an unconditional reality. Thus, the command not to kill is an unconditional statement. It is impossible that the Infinite can be divided into opposing sides who are both willing to kill the other side. It is impossible that the Infinite can give rise to the illusion that it is morally right for one expression of the Infinite to kill another expression of the Infinite.

This illusion can be believed only by the dualistic mind, which is blinded by separation and thus believes in the appearance of two opposing sides. Because the dualistic mind lives in a world where there is nothing infinite, it follows that there is also no infinite way for this mind to define moral law.

***

The dualistic mind cannot define moral law based on the reality of the Infinite. Thus, it will define moral law as a relative concept that is based on conditions in the finite world. This means that one division of the dualistic mind will define moral law in such a way that it makes itself superior to other divisions.

When moral law is defined based on relative conditions in the finite world, it now becomes possible that you can have two sovereigns and two nations arrayed against each other in war, and both sides believe they have the moral law.

Both sides have the firm belief that they have the right to set aside the command not to kill. They both believe they have the right to take the unconditional command not to kill and override it with conditions they have defined based on the appearances of the finite world—their relative definition of moral law.

Yet the command not to kill came from the unconditionality of the Infinite. Thus, there are no conditions in the world of appearances that can override this unconditional command. Thinking this is so causes one to immediately lose the moral law, and it greatly reinforces the illusion of separation.

It is an incomparable reality that when two sovereigns are arrayed against each other in battle, none of them can have the moral law—meaning the non-dualistic moral law that is based on the unconditionality of the Infinite. Of course, both can believe and claim that they do have the moral law—meaning the dualistic moral law that is based on the conditions of the finite world.

Only a fool will be ready to give one's life for such a sovereign.

Only a double fool will believe that giving one's life for a sovereign who does not have the infinite moral law, will lead to fortune in the finite world or entry into the infinite world.

A wise person will know that true fortune and eternal life can be attained only through oneness with the Infinite. Thus, a wise person will know that one has an infinite moral obligation to refuse to fight for a sovereign who claims the finite moral law. Only by refusing to fight in a conditional battle, can one secure one's unconditional survival.

Thinking that eternal life can be attained by entering the consciousness of death is a most dangerous illusion.

The dualistic mind says:

> **(2) Which of the two generals has most ability? (3) With whom lies the advantages derived from Heaven and Earth? (4) On which side is discipline most rigorously enforced? (5) Which army is stronger? (6) On which side are officers and men more highly trained? (7) In which army is there the greater constancy both in reward and punishment?**
> **By means of these seven considerations I can forecast victory or defeat.**

The non-dualistic mind says:

It is true that by deliberating the conditions of the armies, victory and defeat in a finite battle can often be ascertained. Yet the non-dualistic mind can forecast victory and defeat from an incomparable perspective.

Engaging in a finite battle might lead to a finite victory, but such a victory cannot lead to permanent gain or ultimate survival. For when the victory is attained in the finite world of duality, the victory itself will generate an energy impulse. And in the finite world, every impulse has an opposite impulse; every action has an opposite *re*-action.

Any victory attained in a finite battle will automatically and inevitably create an impulse that precipitates the next conflict. Even if you win a victory in a finite battle, it is inevitable that your fortune and survival will soon be threatened by another finite enemy.

Surely, you can keep fighting such finite battles, and you might even be victorious in many of them. But as long as you are engaged in finite battles, you can never escape the possibility of defeat and loss.

When your energies and attention are always engaged in fighting a battle or preparing for the next battle, can it really be said that you have true fortune and true survival? Can it really be said that you have true life? Or are you simply one of the living dead?

Is it not, then, wiser to raise one's mind above the dualistic struggle and discover how to precipitate incomparable abundance directly from the Infinite? Is it not wiser to seek everything from the infinite source, so that there is no need to obtain anything through force?

Thereby, one can attain abundance without generating an opposing impulse. Thus, one's abundance will not be threatened and one's survival has no finite boundary.

Is it not the greater wisdom, then, to pursue understanding of how to draw from the Infinite, rather than letting one's life be consumed by learning how to win a temporary victory in the inconsequential finite struggle?

The dualistic mind says:

The general that hearkens to my counsel and acts upon it, will conquer: let such a one be retained in command! The general that hearkens not to my counsel nor acts upon it, will suffer defeat: let such a one be dismissed!

30

The non-dualistic mind says:

Those who hearken to the counsel of the dualistic mind might conquer a finite army, even gain a finite advantage. Yet they will inevitably suffer ultimate defeat, for they will remain separated from the abundant life of the Infinite.

Those who hearken to the counsel of the dualistic mind, have dismissed themselves from participation in the abundant life. For this life can be attained only by dismissing the dualistic mind and basing one's life on the incomparable wisdom of the Infinite.

Let such unwise ones be dismissed from positions that can influence the lives of individuals, organizations, nations or the planet as a whole.

The dualistic mind says:

While heeding the profit of my counsel, avail yourself also of any helpful circumstances over and beyond the ordinary rules.

According as circumstances are favorable, one should modify one's plans.

The non-dualistic mind says:

Why not avail oneself of the helpful circumstances that lead to an understanding of and union with the Infinite? Why not go beyond all finite rules and modify one's life plans based on the realization that the most favorable circumstances can be obtained only through union with the Infinite?

The dualistic mind says:

All warfare is based on deception.

The non-dualistic mind says:

Here the dualistic mind has spoken a truth.

What is not being said is that in order to do something to another, one must first do the same to oneself.

In order to deceive another, one must first deceive oneself.

In order to kill another, one must first kill a part of oneself.

There is no deceit in the Infinite. Thus, deceit is possible only in the dualistic mind that thinks it is separated from the Infinite. In order to deceive another person, one must make use of the dualistic mind. Yet any use of the dualistic mind comes with a price.

In order to use this mind, you must enter into and become one with the dualistic mind. And you cannot remain united with the Infinite and at the same time be one with the dualistic mind. For no person can serve two masters.

It is impossible to enter the dualistic mind without becoming blinded by its illusions. Thinking one can make use of duality to deceive others and avoid being deceived oneself is the height of folly.

The dualistic mind says:

Hence, when able to attack, we must seem unable; when using our forces, we must seem in-

active; when we are near, we must make the enemy believe we are far away; when far away, we must make him believe we are near.

The non-dualistic mind says:

By engaging in such deceitful measures directed at the enemy, you only bind yourself more to the mind of duality. Thus, for every measure you take in order to deceive the enemy, you bind yourself even more firmly to the mind of deceit.

Who then is really being deceived—the enemy or you? Or is it, perhaps, that both are deceived?

The dualistic mind says:

Now the general who wins a battle makes many calculations in his temple ere the battle is fought. The general who loses a battle makes but few calculations beforehand. Thus do many calculations lead to victory, and few calculations to defeat: how much more no calculation at all! It is by attention to this point that I can foresee who is likely to win or lose.

The non-dualistic mind says:

It is not the quantity of calculations that leads to victory, but the quality of calculations.

True victory can be achieved only by making the incomparable calculations that lead one to see the folly of any dualistic battle. This causes one to connect to the reality that true fortune and true survival can be attained only by rising above the dualistic struggle and reuniting with the Infinite.

Thus, one abandons all finite calculations and focuses all of one's attention and energy on attaining oneness with the Infinite.

The ultimate preparation for non-war is to remove the beam of duality from one's own eye. By allowing that beam to remain, one will inevitably be pulled into the dualistic struggle—perhaps while thinking one is fighting for a just cause.

The only just cause is the cause of the Infinite, which is to awaken all people from the illusion of separation. This cause can never be advanced through a dualistic battle in the finite world.

Death cannot be overcome by bringing more death.

Death can be overcome *only* by bringing LIFE, the incomparable life of the Infinite.

Chapter 2.
Waging Non-war

The dualistic mind says:

When you engage in actual fighting, if victory is long in coming, then men's weapons will grow dull and their ardor will be dampened. If you lay siege to a town, you will exhaust your strength.

The non-dualistic mind says:

Those who engage in finite battles, and achieve a swift victory, will often be so drunk with victory that they mindlessly keep fighting other battles until they are destroyed. Those who have engaged in the finite struggle, and have found that victory is long in coming, have an excellent opportunity to step back and reconsider their approach.

There are two ways open. One way is to hold on to the belief that victory is right around the corner. This will lead one to focus on how to attain the finite advantage that will enable one to win a finite victory over a finite enemy.

While this is indeed possible, one might consider the irony. Most people who engage in a finite battle believe they do so because they have the moral law. This is based on the belief that the enemy represents evil and is so bad that war is a justified means to the end of freeing oneself or the world from the evil of the enemy.

Yet the stark reality of war is that in order to defeat a ruthless enemy, one has to be willing to become more ruthless than the enemy. So in order to defeat an enemy who is steeped in the consciousness of duality, one has to become even better at using the consciousness of duality.

Is it not an irony that people can believe they have the moral law because the enemy is evil, when in reality they can defeat that enemy only by becoming more evil than the enemy? Is it not an even greater irony that people can make themselves worse than the evil they claim to be fighting, yet still believe they have retained the moral law?

The wise ones step back and realize there is a higher way. The higher way is to realize that in a finite battle, your victory will always depend on your ability or willingness to destroy others. Your victory will always be opposed by others, and even if you win a battle, it will only be a temporary victory.

The higher way is to realize that incomparable victory can be achieved only through union with the Infinite. And your union with the Infinite does not depend on other people or any condition in the finite world. Your ultimate victory depends only on yourself and your willingness to rise above the dualistic mind. For the kingdom of the Infinite is within you.

Is it not better to fight a battle where one's victory does not depend upon other people and cannot be opposed by any condition outside oneself?

Of course, this requires one to look at the conditions *within* oneself. Which then requires one to stop using an external enemy as an excuse for *not* looking for the beam in one's own eye.

The dualistic mind says:

There is no instance of a country having benefitted from prolonged warfare.

The non-dualistic mind says:

Again, the dualistic mind has spoken a truth, yet this truth is used only to argue for a swift victory in a finite battle. The greater wisdom is to see that even the swiftest victory will inevitably set the stage for the next dualistic battle.

Any nation that engages in any finite battle, will inescapably be in a state of prolonged warfare. In fact, any nation blinded by the consciousness of duality, will be in a state of perpetual warfare.

The greater wisdom is to see that no nation can benefit from being in this state of perpetual war. Incomparable benefit is for a nation to raise itself above the dualistic mind that is the source of all warfare.

Incomparable benefit can be achieved only through union with the Infinite.

The dualistic mind says:

It is only one who is thoroughly acquainted with the evils of war that can thoroughly understand the profitable way of carrying it on.

The non-dualistic mind says:

Here, the dualistic mind has reinforced the point that in order to defeat an enemy, one must become more evil than the enemy. Only by becoming more skilled at making use of the evils of war, can one carry on the war profitably and defeat the enemy.

The greater wisdom is to realize that no true profit can be gained from being acquainted with and using the evils of war. For in being willing to use such evils, one will only reinforce the barrier in the mind that separates oneself from the Infinite.

The greater wisdom is to realize that true profit can be attained only by raising oneself above the consciousness in which the end seems to justify the means. Consider how many wars have been fought in which both sides believed the enemy was so evil that it was necessary, even justified, to use the most evil means to defeat the enemy.

Consider the double irony that both sides are willing to use the most evil means available to them, while still claiming to have the moral law.

Those who want true benefit and eternal life must abandon the illusion that even if one battle is lost, surely benefit will come in the next battle. They must raise themselves above the dualistic illusions and seek incomparable benefit directly from the Infinite.

The dualistic mind says:

Now in order to kill the enemy, our men must be roused to anger; that there may be advantage

from defeating the enemy, they must have their rewards.

The non-dualistic mind says:

While the dualistic mind is not wise, it is not unintelligent. It knows well the conditions of the finite world, and thus it knows how to use these conditions to attain what it believes is an advantage.

The dualistic mind knows that the Infinite has written its laws in the inward parts of its offspring. Thus, all people have an inner recognition of the validity of the command not to kill. In order to get people to violate this command, the dualistic mind must find a way to make them think that killing is necessary or justified.

The dualistic mind knows that anger is the most powerful force that will cause people to disregard the command not to kill. Thus, before any war, the dualistic mind uses deception to build anger by portraying the enemy as evil.

The wise person sees through this manipulation from the dualistic mind. The wise person sees that anger is a most dangerous state of mind, because it makes one vulnerable to the illusion that committing an evil act is unavoidable or even justified.

The wise person knows that by engaging in anger, one only reinforces the separation between oneself and the Infinite. The stronger the anger, the stronger the separation.

The non-dualistic truth is that *no* benefit can ever be gained from engaging in anger. Anger is *never* justified and is *always* based on the illusions and conditions of duality. The effect of anger is *always* to bind oneself more firmly to the dualistic mind, keeping oneself separated from the Infinite.

A wise person therefore sees clearly that every effort must be made to avoid engaging in the consciousness of anger. One must be on guard and refuse the energy of anger an entry into the energy field of one's mind.

This can be achieved only through constant vigilance against the subtlety of the dualistic temptations. For the dualistic mind has created innumerable and very subtle temptations that seem to justify anger. Only by striving to reconnect oneself to the non-dualistic reality of the Infinite, can one avoid succumbing to the temptations of anger.

For when one knows the reality of the Infinite, one knows that there is no anger in the Infinite. Anger springs from the illusion of separation, which gives rises to opposing forces and the fear of loss. This is what gives rise to the illusion that one can be violated by someone else, that this should not happen and that the unavoidable or justifiable reaction is anger, leading to an all-consuming desire to destroy the enemy.

***

Some people are quickly roused to anger, for they have allowed the energies of anger to accumulate in their energy fields. Others are difficult to rouse to anger, so the dualistic mind must seek to motivate them through the promise of a reward.

The unwise quickly fall prey to the temptation to believe that they will obtain a reward from defeating a finite enemy. The most unwise seek a material reward, and this can often be attained through the spoils of war.

Yet such a reward is temporary, for it is an eternal truth that those who live by the sword shall die by the sword. The reason being that any reward attained through force will inevitably generate an opposing impulse that will prevent one from keeping the reward for long.

Some people are more wise and cannot be roused by anger nor tempted by the promise of a material reward. Yet some of them can be tempted by the promise of an immaterial reward. This might be the reward of seeing their finite expression of truth win the battle against another finite expression of truth. Or it may be the promise that by destroying a finite enemy on Earth, they will obtain some eternal reward in Heaven.

The truly wise see that no eternal reward can ever be obtained through fighting a finite battle. For the non-dualistic mind sees that the Earth is finite, so if one is to obtain an everlasting reward, that reward must be obtained in a world that is beyond the finite. And how can a finite measure ever secure one's entry into the infinite realm?

Those who engage in a finite battle to destroy a finite enemy demonstrate that they are trapped in the dualistic mind that is based on separation. There can be no separation in the infinite world, and thus those trapped in the consciousness of separation simply cannot enter the infinite world of Heaven. And if they cannot enter Heaven, how could they possibly receive a reward in Heaven?

The wise ones see that the promise of a reward made by the dualistic mind is a false promise. The most subtle lie of all is the promise that committing a finite evil will lead to an infinite reward. No lasting reward can ever come from any finite measure.

The wise ones rise above the quest to secure any reward through finite measures. They instead focus their attention and energies on how to obtain an incomparable reward through union with the Infinite.

The wise person does not drink from a stale puddle, but goes to the living spring itself.

The dualistic mind says:

In war, then, let your great object be victory, not lengthy campaigns.

The non-dualistic mind says:

In non-war, then, let your object be to rise above the inconsequential campaign of seeking a finite victory over a finite enemy. Let your object be to attain the incomparable victory that is not in opposition to defeat.

For in union with the Infinite one transcends all duality. And when there is no duality, victory cannot have an opposite. Thus, victory will be ever-lasting. This is the incomparable victory of the Infinite.

The dualistic mind says:

Thus it may be known that the leader of armies is the arbiter of the people's fate, the man on whom it depends whether the nation shall be in peace or in peril.

The non-dualistic mind says:

Again, the dualistic mind has spoken a partial truth. Yet the greater wisdom is that when the leader of a nation has created an army, that leader has already put the nation in peril.

How then can peace be obtained? Only by a critical mass of the people raising themselves above the consciousness of duality. They can then expose the duality of the leader and realign their nation with the reality of the Infinite.

For a nation to escape peril and attain peace, it is vital that a critical mass of its citizens become practitioners of the art of non-war.

Only then can the nation escape the cycle of sending dualistic impulses into the cosmic mirror, impulses that will be returned as material circumstances in which the nation has to fight a finite enemy. Fortunate, indeed, are those nations in which the practitioners of non-war are strong enough to pull the people beyond the downward pull of the forces of war.

Only such nations can send impulses into the cosmic mirror that will be returned as circumstances that lead to peace and prosperity.

Chapter 3.
Non-attack by Incomparable Stratagem

The dualistic mind says:

In the practical art of war, the best thing of all is to take the enemy's country whole and intact; to shatter and destroy it is not so good.

The non-dualistic mind says:

While it is better to take a country whole than to destroy it, this is still only the lesser of two evils. The best thing of all is to rise above the dualistic stratagem of the divided mind and employ the incomparable stratagem of the undivided mind.

What, then, is the incomparable stratagem?

The non-dualistic stratagem begins with the recognition that the Infinite is the source of all that is in existence. However, a subtle – but all-important – distinction must be made.

Saying that everything in the finite world owes its existence to the Infinite is not the same as saying that all things in the finite world were created by or designed in accordance with the intent, vision and laws of the Infinite.

The creative process began when the Infinite expressed itself as a substance that can take on any form. This substance may be called light, as in "Let there be Light," or it may be called energy, as in $E=mc^2$.

Both religion and science have recognized that the basis for all form is a formless, non-differentiated substance that has the potential to take on any distinct form.

Yet this light or energy does not take on form by itself. Creation occurs only when a self-aware being with creative abilities forms a mental image and superimposes it upon the light, causing a portion of the undifferentiated light to coalesce or manifest as a distinct form.

Planet Earth was given form by creative beings who were one with the Infinite. Residing in a realm beyond the material world, they formed the mental image of what the Earth would be like. They then used their creative powers to cause the undifferentiated light to coalesce around the image. Thereby, the light was lowered into the vibrational spectrum of the material universe, and the physical planet was formed.

After the physical planet was formed, spiritual beings were sent to this planet to take on physical bodies and use the Earth as a platform for learning how to use the creative powers of their minds. These beings were created in the image and after the likeness of the Infinite. This does not refer to the physical body but to the fact that people's minds have the same creative abilities – in kind, but not in intensity – as all beings who are one with the Infinite.

The spiritual beings who descended to Earth were given free will, which means they had two options. One is to seek to learn how to use their creative abilities in unity with the Infinite. Another is to use their creative abilities in separation from the Infinite.

***

It is undeniable that there is conflict and warfare on planet Earth. To the dualistic mind, this is simply inevitable. Rather than speculating on the cause, the dualistic mind is focused on – even reveling in – learning how to win the finite battles.

The non-dualistic mind sees clearly that there can be only one cause of conflict and warfare. The spiritual beings who descended to Earth became ensnared by the serpentine consciousness. They were tempted into accepting the illusion that they are separated from the Infinite—thereby inevitably being separated from each other.

By accepting this self-image, the original spiritual beings became – in their own minds – human beings, who are, by their nature, limited in their creative powers. Many believe they have no direct access to the Infinite, some believe they can access the Infinite only through special leaders or institutions, while still others deny that the Infinite even exists. All deny that the kingdom of the Infinite is within them.

All of these forms of self-denial are illusions, but they seem real to the mind that is blinded by duality and thus has not learned to question the fundamental illusion of duality, namely that there can be divisions in and separation from the Infinite.

The non-dualistic mind sees that after spiritual beings fell into the twilight zone of duality, they did not lose their creative powers, although these powers were – mercifully – reduced in strength. Human beings are still spiritual beings who were created in the image and likeness of the Infinite. Thus, they are still using the power of their minds to create. Only, they now do so through the filter of duality, and they do so with diminished power.

Over the ages, human beings have collectively used their creative powers to formulate mental images that are out of harmony with the abundant life of the Infinite. Thus, they have created images of separation and division. This causes them to congregate into separate groups that believe they are in opposition to other groups.

Human beings believe their self-centered mental images can give them some type of gain and even ensure their survival. Yet selfish images can only reduce the total amount of abundance available on Earth and thus they impoverish everyone.

It is an eternal law that those who seek to preserve their separate lives will lose them.

***

The illusion of gain for the separate self is the basic mechanism behind all war. Over the ages, this mechanism has generated an intricate web of dualistic illusions. This is the cause behind the observable fact that most people are born into a group that sees itself as being in opposition to another group, perhaps even in opposition to all other groups because its members are superior to all other human beings.

What are the effects of this web of illusions? It is that life on Earth has become a struggle that has fallen far below the level of abundance at which the planet was created. This is the reason behind the fact that most human religions contain a myth about some prior edenic state from which human beings have fallen.

The non-dualistic reality is that human beings were not cast out of paradise. They cast themselves out by partaking of the fruit of dualistic knowledge, the knowledge of relative good and relative evil. The true paradise is the Circle of Oneness of the Infinite. And since there can be no divisions in infinity, those who accept the mental illusion of separation must of necessity leave the Circle of Oneness.

Because there can be no division in the Infinite, this departure is not an actual departure. The Infinite is everywhere, so how can one find a place where the Infinite is not? Yet because human beings were given free will and the ability to create mental images, they can create the mental image of separation.

Once people have identified themselves with and as such a separate self, they can no longer access the Infinite from within themselves. They can no longer bring forth wisdom directly from the Infinite and must now base their decisions on the thought systems of this world. Yet because humankind has been in duality for so long, there is currently no thought system that is not affected by, or even based upon, the illusions of duality.

Likewise, people cannot bring forth abundance directly from the Infinite, and thus they are confined to the ongoing struggle for a bigger piece of a finite pie. They have forgotten how to use their inherent creative abilities in bringing forth more energy from the Infinite. And they have forgotten how to use their minds to create mental images that are in harmony with the Infinite and thus lead to the precipitation of sustainable abundance for all—rather than temporary abundance for a select elite.

***

The wise ones now see that there is only one way to change the current state of suffering and warfare. One must seek to awaken people from the illusions of duality and separation. For there will never be peace as long as most human beings are trapped by these illusions and believe them to be real.

This process must begin with oneself. One must be willing to look for the beam of duality in one's own eye. One must do the arduous and subtle work of removing all dualistic illusions from one's own mind and heart, whereby one will reconnect to the Infinite. One will then experience the death of the human identity – the separate identity – and experience a rebirth into a new identity as an extension of the Infinite.

After one has begun to recapture one's true identity, one will see clearly how to help other people do the same. One will also see an essential reality.

By reuniting with the Infinite in oneself, one will recapture one's original creative powers. One can draw wisdom directly from the Infinite within oneself and use it to form mental images that enhance not only oneself but enhance all life. By participating in this flow of life, one will help bring about the overall plan that the Infinite has for Earth. This involves the abundant life for all people.

By thus multiplying one's talents, one will receive a true and sustainable reward directly from the Infinite. By being faithful over a few creative powers – using them for the growth of all – one will be made ruler over greater creative powers.

In the beginning, such an awakened person might focus on its own growth and be content to experiment with its newfound powers. Yet eventually, a wise being will begin to see a bigger picture.

There will come the realization that if one is an individualization of the Infinite, then other human beings are also individualizations of the Infinite. And if all are expressions of the Infinite, then individuality is not the same as separation. Thus, the differences of individuality do not have to lead to competition and conflict.

This leads to the realization that an awakened being truly can have no enemies. For when it is recognized that all came from the Infinite, and that all separation is an illusion, then the concept of enemies is also an illusion.

***

An awakened being might still meet people who are blinded by the illusions of duality and thus see themselves as enemies of the awakened person. Yet the awakened person will refuse to confirm this illusion and will thus refuse to enter into a dualistic conflict. Instead, the awakened person will focus its efforts on awakening other people to the reality of the Infinite.

It now becomes clear why the stratagem of the dualistic mind is a self-destructive stratagem. It is focused on deceiving and subverting the enemy by using the illusions of the dualistic mind with greater skill than the enemy. If subversion cannot be attained, then force will be used to destroy the enemy—or oneself.

The effect of such a stratagem is that it will become impossible to expand the amount of abundance that exists. And if violent conflict ensues, cities might be destroyed, people killed and thus the amount of wealth will be reduced.

The awakened person realizes that he or she is an expression of the Infinite. As such, one can access the Infinite directly. And by bringing forth wisdom and energy from the infinite supply, one can expand the total amount of abundance that is available on Earth. Thus, one can enrich oneself without taking from anyone else.

The awakened person sees the eternal truth that what is best for oneself is what is best for the larger self, the All. Only by working for raising up the All, will one truly enrich oneself. For inasmuch as you have done it to the least of the brethren, you have done it to the Infinite. Only by seeking to enrich others, will you truly enrich yourself.

The awakened being also realizes that even though it can draw from the Infinite, it is still only an individual expression. And the amount of wisdom and energy that can flow through one mind will always be limited. As long as an awakened person is tapping only its own creative powers, there will be a limit to how much abundance can be created.

To bring forth even greater abundance, one awakened being must come together with another awakened being. For when two or three are gathered in the name of the Infinite, there will be the Presence of Abundance in the midst of them.

This collective opening will not be only an addition of the creative power of the individual minds. It will be an exponential multiplication. Two people can precipitate not simply twice as much abundance as one, but many times more.

***

The awakened being sees that the superior stratagem is *not* to seek to deceive and subdue the enemy. The superior stratagem is to use the reality of the Infinite to overcome the illusion that other people are enemies.

The greatest advantage cannot be attained by subduing or destroying other people. The greatest advantage can be attained only by awakening other people to the reality of the Infinite.

An awakened being is one who has discovered the Infinite within itself. Such a being also sees the Infinite in other people. The awakened being knows that if these unawakened people became awakened, they would discover the Infinite within themselves also.

And when several people have all discovered the Infinite within themselves, they can come together in true unity—their individual beings united through their connection to the Infinite. Thereby, they can bring forth infinitely more creative power and enrich not only themselves but all life on Earth.

They can make a contribution to bringing the Earth back to its original state, in which the abundant life was available to all. They can then build upon the original foundation and bring forth even more abundance. For there is virtually no limit to how much wisdom and energy can be brought forth when a large number of awakened beings come together in true oneness.

52

The Infinite is One, which is why it is infinite. For when divisions exist, none of them can be infinite. Individual expressions of the Infinite were created within the Circle of Oneness and thus had the abundant life. By separating themselves from that circle, they have lost the abundant life. Yet by overcoming that separation – uniting their individual beings in oneness – they again gain access to the abundant life of the One.

When the many become as one, they become the One.

To the awakened person the superior stratagem is to use the wisdom, love and power of the Infinite to awaken those who are still trapped in the illusions of duality.

If you can awaken an enemy to the presence of the Infinite within itself, then the enemy will become your partner. And the multiplication of your collective efforts will enrich both of you beyond what any of you could achieve alone.

Together you can go beyond the finite resources that foster competition and conflict. Instead of competing for a larger slice of a limited pie, you can expand the pie beyond the imagination of most people.

This is the non-dualistic stratagem, and it is in all ways far superior to the dualistic stratagem. It is the only way to bring forth incomparable abundance and attain eternal life.

The dualistic mind says:

Hence to fight and conquer in all your battles is not supreme excellence; supreme excellence consists in breaking the enemy's resistance without fighting.

The non-dualistic mind says:

Inevitably, the dualistic mind will be unable to fathom the non-dualistic stratagem. People who are still blinded by duality will deny the validity of this stratagem. The dualistic mind – working through them – will come up with innumerable arguments against it.

This is because the dualistic mind will never overcome the separation out of which it was born. Separation from the Infinite is death.

Death can never overcome death.

Death can only be overcome by Life.

Once dead, one must be reborn in order to experience life. Yet rebirth must be preceded by the death of the separate self.

One can overcome the consciousness of death only by being reborn into the consciousness of Life. Hereby, the separate self is allowed to die and the person is reborn to its original identity as an individualization of the Infinite.

Once a self-aware being accepts the illusion of separation, a separate self is born, and this separate self believes it is merely a human being. The dualistic mind wants all people to believe that they are nothing more than human beings, that they must forever remain separated from the Infinite.

Yet every self-aware being is more than the separate self. The conscious self of any person has the potential to awaken from the illusion of separation, to see the separate self as unreal and then to allow that separate self to die instead of seeking to preserve it through the dualistic struggle. And when the separate self dies, the conscious self is reborn into its original identity as an extension of the Infinite.

Those who seek to save their finite lives, will lose their infinite lives. Yet those who are willing to lose their separate lives for the sake of the Infinite, will indeed find eternal life by discovering the kingdom of the Infinite within themselves.

***

The consciousness of death has no ability to choose, like a computer cannot choose to change its own programming. Only self-aware beings have a choice between the consciousness of death and the consciousness of Life.

The consciousness of death will – indefinitely – resist the non-dualistic stratagem. The practitioners of the art of non-war understand why this is so and are unmoved. The key to being unmoved by the dualistic mind is to understand the nature of resistance.

The dualistic mind is based on separation. Separation is based on resistance to the Infinite and the River of Life that is the flow of infinity through finite forms.

The Infinite has created the finite world for the purpose of giving self-aware extensions of itself the opportunity to grow in awareness by traveling from a finite state toward union with the Infinite.

In the original blueprint, everything in the finite world is designed to facilitate this journey from finite to infinite. The totality of the finite world is not static but forms a mighty stream – a River of Life – that flows toward infinity like a river flows toward union with the ocean. If this was not so, how could the material universe continue to expand?

The material universe is one part of the finite world—the only part visible to the dualistic mind. The material universe is like the tip of the iceberg formed by the entire world of form. An iceberg has most of its mass under the surface of the water, being carried along with the ocean currents—even against the wind that blows on the surface. So also is the material universe carried along by the River of Life that brings it ever closer to infinity.

Because of free will, self-aware beings in the material universe can resist this natural flow toward infinity. They can cling to a particular finite expression and seek to preserve it. They can seek to possess what is given freely by the Infinite.

In doing so, they have to resist the natural flow that would have transformed any finite expression into a more abundant form. This requires constant resistance, and most people are like a beggar who is clinging to his begging bowl while refusing the prince who offers to trade it for a palace.

The resistance to the natural flow of abundance will inevitably create an opposing dualistic force that is aimed at breaking down the resistance, so that the self-aware being can, once again, be free to flow with the River of Life.

Anything that stands still and seeks to hold on to a finite form, will inevitably create an opposing force. The more one resists, the stronger the opposing force becomes, and it is only a matter of time before it becomes stronger than the physical and mental powers of the self-aware being.

A group of self-aware beings can combine their mental powers in holding on to a finite form. They can slow down the forward movement of their environment – even an entire planet – and turn it into a closed sphere that is still inside the River of Life but moving at a slower rate than the river itself.

Yet even this will create an opposing force, and it will eventually break down the finite structures to which people cling. Those who seek to preserve their finite form of life by resisting the River of Life, will inevitably lose that finite life.

This principle is demonstrated by modern science in the second law of thermodynamics. It states that in a closed system, resistance – caused by opposing forces – will increase until the organized structures that generate the resistance are broken down and the closed system has destroyed itself.

The ultimate definition of a closed system is one that is separated from the Infinite, separated from the River of Life. Because so many human beings have been blinded by duality for so long, the Earth is close to being such a closed system. This fact can explain all of the limitations and suffering seen on this planet.

**

Practitioners of the art of non-war understand the nature and effects of resistance. They see that by resisting the natural flow of the River of Life, one will inevitably become trapped in a perpetual struggle against an opposing force. This will turn one into a closed system that is eventually destroyed by its internal resistance.

One can continue in this struggle until one's energies and opportunity is depleted. Or one can decide that one has had enough of the struggle and then plunge oneself into the River of Life. Having understood this, the quintessential human choice, practitioners of non-war start by pulling the beam of resistance from their own eyes, and then they immerse themselves in the River of Life.

Once they are in the river, they know that when other people resists them, they do so because they are still trapped in duality. When you are awakened, you see that an unawakened person is not actually resisting *you*, but is truly resisting the River of Life. Such people are driven by internal divisions that cause resistance, and it has nothing to do with you. Thus, you can forgive them, for you see that they know not what they do.

The awakened person sees that when the dualistic mind says, "supreme excellence consists in breaking the enemy's resistance without fighting," it is speaking an illusion.

Numerous are the battles fought between people trapped in duality, each side seeking to break the resistance of the enemy. Yet in reality, both sides are resisting the River of Life, and this can only lead to death. The one who breaks the resistance of the enemy has not achieved true excellence but has only achieved excellence in the ways of death. That person's resistance to the River of Life is simply greater than that of the enemy—who lost because its resistance was not as strong.

The awakened ones know that true excellence is *not* to break the resistance of the enemy but to transform that resistance by awakening the "enemy" to the virtue of flowing with the River of Life. Once both you and your former enemy are flowing with the river, you can unite your efforts and bring forth more abundance than either could achieve alone.

Supreme excellence is to transform the enemy's resistance into union with the River of Life.

The dualistic mind says:

Therefore, the skillful leader subdues the enemy's troops without any fighting; he captures their cities without laying siege to them; he overthrows their kingdom without lengthy operations in the field.

With his forces intact he will dispute the mastery of the Empire, and thus, without losing a man, his triumph will be complete. This is the method of attacking by stratagem.

The non-dualistic mind says:

The truly skillful leader does not dispute the finite mastery of another empire but seeks to transform it into incomparable mastery. An awakened leader is not seeking greater mastery in the art of resistance, the art of war. Such a leader is seeking mastery in the art of non-resistance, the art of non-war, the art of oneness.

An awakened leader knows that if an empire is trapped in the consciousness of resistance, the consciousness of death, it is existing far below its true potential. No sustainable advantage could be gained in conquering such an empire. It is simply not a worthy prize, regardless of its material possessions. The assimilation of such an inferior empire into one's own, would only drag one's own further down into the depths of duality, the valley of the shadow of death.

The wise ruler sees that the superior stratagem is to seek to awaken the other empire to the virtues of non-resistance. Once the empire is flowing with the River of Life and approaching its true potential, the two awakened empires will naturally form a greater union and manifest greater abundance than either could achieve alone.

The dualistic mind says:

Thus we may know that there are five essentials for victory: (1) He will win who knows when to fight and when not to fight; (2) He will win who knows how to handle both superior and inferior forces; (3) He will win whose army is animated by the same spirit throughout all its ranks; (4) He will win who, having prepared himself, waits to take the enemy unprepared.

He will win who has military capacity and is not interfered with by the sovereign.

The non-dualistic mind says:

Thus we may know that there are five essentials for non-dualistic victory:

1. They will win who know never to fight in a finite battle. For fighting springs from resistance, and resistance only separates oneself further from the River of Life. Anything that separates oneself from the river can never lead to incomparable victory.

2. They will win who have transcended the consciousness of duality in which some people are superior and some inferior. There can be no divisions in the Infinite, and thus the concepts of superior and inferior have no reality. When all are flowing with the River of Life – living up to their highest potential – who has any use for the illusion of superiority and inferiority?

3. They will win who are united in the true Spirit of the Infinite. They have overcome the temptation to worship one of the many lesser spirits springing from the consciousness of duality. They have overcome the temptation to put another God before the Infinite and to take unto themselves a graven image, worshiping something in the finite world before the Infinite.

4. They will win who have achieved true preparation, namely oneness with the Infinite, and who seek to extend that oneness to all others.

5. They will win who have transformed their military capacity into the capacity to awaken others to the reality of the Infinite. These are the ones who are working with the only true sovereign, the Infinite.

The dualistic mind says:

Hence the saying: If you know the enemy and know yourself, you need not fear the result of a hundred battles. If you know yourself but not the enemy, for every victory gained you will also suffer a defeat. If you know neither the enemy nor yourself, you will succumb in every battle.

The non-dualistic mind says:

Those trapped in the dualistic mind can never fully know themselves nor know the enemy. For does not the very thought that one has an enemy show that one does not know that one's source is the Infinite? No matter how much finite knowledge one accumulates, one can never escape the dualistic forces that will eventually lead to ruin and death.

When you truly know yourself, you know you are an extension of the Infinite. When you truly know other people, you know they too are extensions of the Infinite. When you truly know the Infinite, you know that none of the divisions in the finite world are ultimately real. Truly knowing yourself and truly knowing your enemy means knowing that all are part of the One Body of the Infinite. Thus, there are no enemies.

When you awaken to the reality of the Infinite, you rise above the consciousness of duality, which means you have escaped the duality of finite victory and defeat. Only by giving up the desire for finite victory, can you escape the inevitability of finite defeat.

The practitioners of the art of non-war have risen above the possibility of finite victory and defeat. They have escaped the illusion in which victory can exist only as the opposite of defeat, and thus every victory sets the stage for a future defeat.

They have come to know the incomparable Victory that has no opposite, for it is based on perpetual oneness with the Infinite.

Chapter 4.
Non-dual Tactical Dispositions

The dualistic mind says:

The good fighters of old first put themselves beyond the possibility of defeat, and then waited for an opportunity of defeating the enemy.

The non-dualistic mind says:

The non-dual fighters of the now first put themselves beyond the possibility of defeat by raising themselves above the duality of finite victory-defeat, merging themselves with the one reality of incomparable Victory.

Having transformed the desire to defeat the enemy into a true desire to awaken the enemy, they do not passively wait for the enemy to awaken. They go out and actively seek to awaken the enemy, transforming the enemy into an equal. Equality will lead to partnership, where the unity of minds will bring forth greater abundance than could be won through any finite struggle.

The dualistic mind says:

To secure ourselves against defeat lies in our own hands, but the opportunity of defeating the enemy is provided by the enemy himself.

Thus the good fighter is able to secure himself against defeat, but cannot make certain of defeating the enemy.

Hence the saying: One may know how to conquer without being able to do it.

The non-dualistic mind says:

Securing oneself against defeat means raising oneself above the consciousness of duality, which is the source of both finite victory and finite defeat. Surely, the key to this transformation lies within one's own mind. It is not dependent upon any external force, philosophy, person or institution in the finite world. It is, however, dependent upon one's inner willingness to let go of the finite self and surrender into oneness with the Infinite.

The practitioners of non-war are able to awaken themselves from the illusions of duality, yet they cannot be sure of awakening others. This is because practitioners of non-war have uncompromising respect for free will. This respect comes from a thorough understanding of free will.

The Infinite individualized itself as finite beings with the capacity of mind to grow towards re-union with the Infinite. The Infinite desires this growth to happen as the result of free choices, where an individual being comes to understand that re-uniting with the Infinite leads to an incomparable advantage. It keeps one in the River of Life, which gives one the abundant life while in the material realm and then the eternal life in the spiritual realm.

An awakened being always seeks unity with the Infinite and is constantly alert toward anything that pulls one away from the River of Life. Yet because free will is truly free, a being has the option to resist the flow of the River of Life by seeking to hold on to a finite form.

64

Making this choice is the right of any self-aware being—but only for a time. The Infinite has given a portion of its own being to every self-aware being, and it does not want a portion of itself to be trapped in the finite world indefinitely.

***

To prevent a self-aware being from remaining trapped in the finite world, the law of free will does not stand alone. It is inseparably linked with the law of cause and effect.

In the finite world, every action has a reaction, meaning that every action produces a consequence, an effect. A self-aware being has the right to perform any action, but it cannot escape experiencing the consequences of its actions.

This is not reward or punishment, for the finite world is designed as a schoolroom rather than a prison. The finite world forms a mirror that will reflect back material circumstances that correspond to the mental impulses sent out by a self-aware being.

The cosmic mirror is capable of producing any type of material circumstances that a self-aware being wants to experience. It has no judgments or opinions. It faithfully reflects back material circumstances that mirror the mental impulses that a self-aware being is sending out.

This is so designed because it gives self-aware beings an opportunity to experience the consequences of their mental states and thus learn how to use the creative powers of their minds. Everything in the world of form is created out of the mind of the Infinite. Self-aware beings are meant to serve as co-creators with the Infinite. Thus, they must learn to create as the Infinite creates—through the powers of the mind.

If a self-aware being fills its mind with thoughts that are based on harmony with the Infinite, the cosmic mirror will reflect back a materially abundant life. If a being fills its mind with images based on separation and duality, the cosmic mirror will reflect back circumstances in which there is a struggle between opposing forces.

An awakened being keeps its mind attuned to the River of Life, and thus the mirror reflects back not only abundance, but a progressive abundance that grows in harmony with the forward movement of the entire world of form. This is the finite growing closer to union with the Infinite.

An unawakened being has allowed its mind to become separated from the harmony and oneness of the River of Life. Its mind has become attuned to the dualistic images born from the illusion of separation. This dualistic world is not dominated by a united flow toward greater abundance. Instead, it is dominated by an ongoing struggle between opposing forces that are constantly diminishing each other, thus leading to progressively lower abundance.

The cosmic mirror makes no judgments of right and wrong. It is designed only to reflect back material conditions that correspond to the mental images that self-aware beings send out. It is content to give any self-aware being – and any group of self-aware beings – the circumstances they say they desire to experience.

How does the cosmic mirror determine what circumstances a self-aware being wants to experience? By examining what the being is sending out, including how it treats other beings.

An awakened being realizes that the admonishment to "Do unto others as you want them to do onto you" is based on a profound understanding of how the finite world is designed. What you do to others signals to the cosmic mirror what circumstances you desire to experience. And the cosmic mirror will faithfully fulfill your wish.

If you send out a mental image based on the reality of the Infinite, the mirror will reason that you want to experience the abundant life for all. If you send out a mental image based on the illusions of duality, the mirror must reason that you want to experience a life that is dominated by the struggle between opposing forces.

An unawakened being does not understand this truth. The reason is that the being has become blinded by the consciousness of separation. This state of mind leads a self-aware being to think that it is separated from the Infinite, perhaps even that the Infinite does not exist.

This leads such a being to believe in the illusion that there is a separation between action and reaction, between actions and consequences. Thus, the being comes to believe in the lie that it can escape experiencing the consequences of its actions. Some even believe in the ultimate lie that actions have no consequences.

When the mirror sends back material circumstances that reflect their internal duality, unawakened beings fail to see this as a self-created condition. Thus, they rebel against it, meaning that they struggle against the struggle. The mirror has only one option, namely to reason that these people want to experience an even more intense struggle. It must comply by giving them material circumstances with more conflict and less abundance.

This is how a downward spiral is created. It will not stop until the people who created it run out of time or take responsibility for themselves and acknowledge the timeless fact that their outer circumstances will not change until they change their state of mind.

Because everything is a creation of the mind, material circumstances are nothing but the reflection of a state of mind. The current suffering and conflict on Earth being a reflection of the state of the collective mind.

***

Practitioners of non-war understand why the illusion of a separation between actions and consequences is so persuasive on Earth. They understand why people who commit selfish acts often seem to reap no immediate consequences.

When a being has attuned its mind perfectly to the River of Life, any mental impulse sent into the cosmic mirror will be instantly reflected back as material circumstances. Such a one can instantly change the water of the finite into the wine of the Infinite.

As a self-aware being begins to attune its mind to the dualistic illusions, an impulse sent into the cosmic mirror will not be reflected back instantly but will be subject to a delay in time. The further a being has descended into duality, the longer it will take before its mental impulses are reflected back as material circumstances.

This is what has given rise to the common belief that the most selfish people can get away with anything and are above the laws of man. Yet such people are not above the laws of the Infinite. To the unawakened mind, the time delay seems like an injustice, yet the awakened mind sees that it is an act of mercy.

Every self-aware being is an extension of the Infinite, for only the Infinite has self-awareness. The Infinite has given all extensions of itself free will, which means that a being can send a mental impulse into the cosmic mirror that will destroy its body when the impulse is reflected back as a material circumstance. The Infinite has no desire to see any extension of itself self-destruct but desires only to see all of them return to union with itself.

When a self-aware being begins to send out mental impulses that are based on the illusions of duality, the return of such impulses is delayed. This gives the being an opportunity to change its consciousness before it reaps the consequences of its former actions.

Compare this to a person who takes out a loan from the bank. There are no payments for ten years, but then the debt and interest has to be paid in full. If the person spends the money wisely, it may multiply the talents and accumulate more money than the loan amount. In that case, paying back the loan will be easy.

Yet if the person refuses to invest wisely, it might squander all the money or go into further debt. Even if the person buries the talents in the ground, there will not be enough to pay the interest. In that case, paying back the loan may be impossible and cause the person to be thrown into jail.

The inescapable reality is that a person who today experiences imperfect circumstances does so as the direct result of imperfect mental impulses sent into the cosmic mirror in the past—often in an unremembered past. The unawakened person refuses to believe this, and must inevitably see itself as a victim of circumstances and forces beyond its control.

Such a person gives away its power to change its future, for the only way to change one's future is to change one's state of mind. Only by sending different mental images into the cosmic mirror, will one experience a different return.

***

Although a selfish person can escape reaping the consequences of its actions for a time, a selfish state of consciousness also has immediate consequences.

Humankind started descending into the illusions of separation and duality in a very distant past. People have sent out selfish impulses for a long time, and the return of such impulses have led to the current conditions of limitations and conflicts.

This has changed the original design of the Earth and precipitated planetary circumstances that cause most people to experience life as an ongoing struggle for limited resources. Unawakened people live in this perpetual struggle, whereas only the awakened ones can raise themselves above it.

The collective mind – existing as a field of mental and emotional energy surrounding the physical planet as the invisible field around a magnet – has huge accumulations of the energies produced by this struggle. These energies

– having been produced by the minds of human beings – exert a magnetic pull on the thoughts and feelings of all inhabitants of the physical planet.

Anyone who engages in selfish actions will open his or her mind to the magnetic pull of these energies, which can quickly overpower the person's mind and make life miserable. This explains why some people become para- lyzed by fear or become consumed by an anger that seems unwarranted by the person's outer circumstances.

This openness to energies from the collective mind is one of the main factors that can explain many mental disor- ders, from depression to suicide. The other factor is the dualistic illusions that turn a person's mind into a house divided against itself.

Those who open their minds to the dualistic illusions, will inevitably attune their minds to the struggle and will thus be pulled into the fray of fighting finite battles against other people. Only an awakened person, who at- tunes its mind to the River of Life, can avoid being pulled into the maelstrom of the dualistic struggle.

Practitioners of non-war understand these facts and thus understand their true role on Earth. The awakened people are not meant to passively watch as their brothers and sis- ters remain stuck in the dualistic struggle. They are meant to serve as examples, so that others can see that there is an alternative to the ongoing struggle.

In serving as examples, it is essential that the practitio- ners of non-war do not fall prey to the many subtle temp- tations that are designed to pull them back into the strug- gle. This can be attained only by those who have an uncompromising respect for the law of free will because they understand the reality written into its design.

***

One of the most subtle and persuasive of all finite temptations is the concept that it is acceptable to do evil that good may come, that the ends can justify the means. This has caused innumerable well-meaning people to believe in the illusion that in order to help or "save" other people, it is acceptable to manipulate their free will by seeking to control their minds.

The essence of the dualistic struggle is that people seek to manipulate the minds of others in order to influence their will. Practitioners of the art of war are constantly seeking for ways to weaken the enemy's defenses in order to take over their empires without using overt force.

The entire purpose for awakening people is to help them escape this struggle. So how could this cause possibly be advanced, if those who claim to support it resort to the same methods as those who are trapped in the struggle?

Believing one can produce good by doing evil shows a lack of wisdom. At least those who acknowledge that they are practitioners of the art of war are honest in admitting that they seek to suppress the will of others through deceit. Yet many dishonestly claim – and sincerely believe – that they are good people who are working for a good cause.

Those who truly work for the cause of the Infinite must do so by respecting the laws of the Infinite, including the law of free will. So how can one claim to be working for the cause of the Infinite, if one is willing to deceive and manipulate the free will of others? This is nothing but hypocrisy, and it is the truth behind the statement that the road to hell is paved with good intentions.

The temptation is subtle. One sees that another person is trapped in duality and is engaged in behavior that is clearly self-destructive. One sees that the person cannot recognize that there is an alternative to the dualistic struggle, cannot fathom the reality of the Infinite.

Since one seemingly cannot help the person see the wisdom of changing his or her behavior, would it not be acceptable to use certain seemingly benign means to manipulate the person into stopping the self-destructive behavior?

This very reasoning has caused groups of people to create elaborate thought systems aimed at scaring people into stopping self-destructive behavior, often based on instilling fear of an eternal torment in hell. Yet what is the value in changing a person's outer behavior without helping the person escape the consciousness of duality?

Fear is a consequence of the dualistic mind, for surely there is no fear in the Infinite. All fear springs from the illusion of separation from the Infinite, which gives rise to the further illusions of lack and loss. A person who changes behavior because of fear is still trapped in duality and will still be sending dualistic mental images into the cosmic mirror.

They might be different images than what the person was sending out before being converted to a fear-based belief system, but they are still dualistic images. So when these images are reflected back by the cosmic mirror, the person will still find itself in the dualistic struggle. There might be a quantitative improvement, but there will be no qualitative improvement.

***

Many people become involved in defending or expanding a fear-based belief system by battling against other fear-based belief systems.

Many people have used a religious, political or materialistic belief system as a justification for entrapping themselves even more firmly in the consciousness of duality, while being entirely convinced that they are working for a good cause and thus are on the road to their definition of salvation.

If one is working for a good cause but influenced by the illusion that the ends can justify the means, then one is still on the broad way that leads to destruction. Only those who abandon the illusions of duality and attune their minds to the Infinite, can discover and follow the straight and narrow way that leads to infinite life.

This explains why it is essential that the practitioners of non-war understand the facts of free will and the design of the cosmic mirror. Only then can they avoid being deceived by their own good intentions. For those who fail to see that their intentions are good only in a dualistic sense, will inevitably become practitioners of the art of war, even while thinking they are working for peace.

The Infinite has no desire to see people become good in the relative, dualistic sense that is in contrast to evil. The Infinite desires people to rise above duality and become good in the sense that has no opposite, for it is one with the undivided state of the Infinite itself. This is incomparable goodness and it is a requirement for practitioners of non-war.

Practitioners of non-war are not seeking to become good human beings. They are seeking to become *more* than human beings through oneness with the Infinite.

***

Practitioners of war find it almost impossible to engage in non-dualistic relationships. Practitioners of non-war express their non-dualistic understanding in their relationships with other people. Practitioners of war seek a win-lose outcome of every situation. Practitioners of non-war seek a win-win outcome of every situation.

Practitioners of non-war fully internalize the truth that they are here *not* to force or deceive other people into making "better" choices. They are here to give other people the opportunity to choose something that is beyond duality. This is done first and foremost by demonstrating a way of life that is beyond the dualistic struggle.

Only those who have raised themselves beyond the illusions and temptations of the dualistic mind, can hope to help others escape the dualistic struggle. For only when you remove the beam of duality from your own eye, will you see clearly how to help others remove that same beam from their eyes.

One's first concern must be to always be true to oneself, meaning one's infinite Self. Do not seek to force others into accepting your understanding. Do not allow others to stop you from expressing who you are. Do not focus on changing other people but focus on being your true self and expressing your infinite individuality through your finite identity.

In being who you are as an expression of the Infinite, you can remain centered and at peace even in the midst of intense situations. This will cause others to wonder, and some will ask how you are able to maintain peace. You can then share your truth with them, yet leave it completely up to them how they respond. You can continue to work with such people as long as they are open to a non-dualistic understanding.

You will meet some people who are so burdened by the dualistic struggle that they cannot even see that you have the peace that they lack. Or perhaps they are so blinded by dualistic illusions that they cannot even formulate a question.

To such people you can offer a cup of cold water in the name of the Infinite by explaining that there is an alternative to the dualistic struggle. Yet you must be very clear in leaving it completely up to them whether they will drink of the cup that contains the life-giving water of the Infinite, or whether they will continue to drink of the cup that contains the bitter gall of duality.

You will meet many people who will ignore or reject anything you offer them. Do not let this stop you from being who you are. To accomplish this, you must stay out of both of the two dualistic reactions. One is to become discouraged and stop expressing who you are, the other is to become fanatical and seek to force others into listening to you or following you.

If you offer someone a cup of cold water and they reject it, you simply remain non-attached and let them be. Instead, you focus your attention on those who do respond. If someone responds for a time, yet will not follow you all the way to the River of Life, you again do not react in a dualistic way. You allow them to follow their own path while continuing to follow yours.

The first rule is to focus on those who are open to a higher understanding, while leaving others to reap their own experiences from the cosmic mirror. However, there will be some who are not content to let you be and who will aggressively seek to silence you. To avoid being tempted to engage in a dualistic struggle with such people, one must understand a deeper truth about the law of free will.

***

The Infinite created self-aware, individualized extensions of itself and sent them into the finite world. The purpose was to give them an opportunity to learn how to use their creative powers. Hereby, they can help co-create the kingdom of the Infinite in the finite world, raising the finite world towards infinity.

Self-aware beings start out with an individualized sense of identity, and they have creative powers that are similar – in quality but not in quantity – to the powers of the Infinite. By expanding their attunement with the Infinite, self-aware beings can expand their creative powers, eventually approaching those of the Infinite.

Yet the expansion in creative power can only happen based on an expansion of one's sense of self. Those who use their creative powers to benefit the All will increase their creative powers. Those who become trapped in the illusions of duality – and begin to use their creative powers to benefit the separate self – will decrease their creative power. They will no longer be able to precipitate abundance directly from the Infinite, but must now take it from others through deceit or force.

All self-aware beings are on a journey from a finite sense of self to an infinite sense of self. This requires the expansion of one's sense of self, from the individual – potentially separate – sense of self to a sense of oneness with the Infinite and through that oneness with all life.

When oneness with the One Self of the All is achieved, there is still individuality but it is not separate from the whole. This is not a loss of individuality but the ultimate expansion of individuality.

This path has been taught or demonstrated by the awakened ones who have been sent to Earth in many disguises, such as Lao Tzu, Confucius, the Buddha, Jesus, Mohammed and many others, known or unknown.

All self-aware beings have been given free will, so they have the right to design their life's journey any way they want, seeking any type of experience they desire along the way. Yet because it is a journey through the finite world, the journey itself must have a finite limit—it cannot go on forever. Immortality cannot be achieved in the finite world.

Immortality can be achieved only by transcending the finite world, by transcending the separate, finite sense of self. Only the selfless can enter the infinite world beyond the finite. The consequence is that each self-aware being starts out with a finite, but very long, time span before the end of which it must return to the Infinite.

A self-aware being also starts out with a certain quantity of creative powers. The being has free will and can choose to use these powers any way it wants, yet it cannot choose to avoid experiencing the consequences of its creative actions. The cosmic mirror will inevitably reflect back any impulse sent into it.

If a being multiplies its talents by seeking to bring forth greater abundance for all life, then its creative powers will be multiplied. If a being falls prey to the illusion of a separate self and uses its powers to give an advantage to the separate self by taking from other forms of life, then that being will have its creative powers reduced.

Those who fall prey to the temptation to act in selfish ways will decrease their creative powers. This will also decrease the time span they have left for their return, for if you have less creative powers, how can you sustain yourself on a long journey?

All self-aware beings have free will. A selfish act is one where you interfere with the free will of others. You have the right to do anything you want—as long as it affects only yourself. If your actions interfere with the freedom of others, such actions will decrease your opportunity to remain on Earth.

Of course, because the Earth is an interconnected system, any action committed by any being on Earth affects the whole. That is why it is said that no human is an island and that there are no free lunches.

***

The practitioners of war have fallen prey to one of the many dualistic illusions that make it seem necessary or even justified to violate the free will of others. Having been awakened from the dualistic illusions, the practitioners of non-war know that it is *never* justified to violate the free will of others. Thus, they have the basis for truly non-dualistic relationships:

- Your primary goal is to awaken others. You work with those who respond by seeking to enlighten them so they can make better choices.

- With those who are too burdened to respond, you seek to demonstrate to them that there is a better way than the broad way of duality. If they respond, you seek to enlighten them. If they do not respond, you respect their free will and their right to follow their own path. Thus, you leave them alone.

- With those who seek to aggressively silence you, you respond in a non-dualistic manner by following the timeless advice to turn the other cheek.

Turning the other cheek is not a passive measure, but it does have two sides. One is to challenge the illusions that are blinding the aggressors without fighting the aggressors themselves. The other is to allow the aggressors to violate you – over and over again, if necessary – in order to cause them to bring about their own judgment, thereby decreasing both their creative powers and the time they have left on Earth.

By challenging the illusions of the aggressors, you might not awaken the aggressors themselves, but you might awaken others who have blindly followed the aggressors. And by turning the other cheek, you hasten the day when the aggressors will run out of opportunity, whereby the Earth will be set free from the burden of such selfish beings.

If you respond to an aggressor by either defending yourself or fighting back, you will only enter the dualistic struggle and thereby perpetuate that struggle. If you respond in a non-dualistic manner by challenging the illusions or turning the other cheek, you do not perpetuate the dualistic struggle.

Practitioners of non-war know that they are not working against other people, for even the aggressors are self-aware extensions of the Infinite—they have simply become blinded by dualistic illusions and have created a separate self that now controls their minds. The real cause is to diminish the consciousness, the collective mind, of duality that has engulfed the entire planet and has pulled many people into following it blindly.

If you respond dualistically, you only add to the magnetic, gravitational pull of the consciousness of duality. When you respond non-dualistically, you diminish that pull, thus making it easier for other people to open their eyes and see the folly of duality and the incomparable reward of non-duality. Setting others free from the blindness of duality is the overall goal for all practitioners of non-war.

The dualistic mind says:

Security against defeat implies defensive tactics; ability to defeat the enemy means taking the offensive.

Standing on the defensive indicates insufficient strength; attacking, a superabundance of strength.

The non-dualistic mind says:

Practitioners of non-war apply neither defensive nor offensive tactics. They know that both defensive and offensive actions are part of the dualistic struggle.

Having been awakened from the illusions of duality, practitioners of non-war stay on the middle way that is above and beyond all dualistic extremes.

They have neither insufficient finite strength nor a superabundance of finite strength. They have the incomparable strength that comes only from oneness with the Infinite.

The dualistic mind says:

The general who is skilled in defense hides in the most secret recesses of the Earth; he who is skilled in attack flashes forth from the topmost heights of Heaven. Thus on the one hand we have ability to protect ourselves; on the other, a victory that is complete.

The non-dualistic mind says:

Practitioners of non-war seek neither to hide in the Earth nor do they seek to flash forth from a finite Heaven. They seek the true Heaven of the Infinite that is unfathomable, thus unreachable, to the dualistic mind.

Practitioners of non-war seek neither protection from finite aggression nor victory in a finite battle. Being above victory and defeat, they find the incomparable peace that can come only from union with the Infinite.

The dualistic mind says:

What the ancients called a clever fighter is one who not only wins, but excels in winning with ease. He wins his battles by making no mistakes. Making no mistakes is what establishes the certainty of victory, for it means conquering an enemy that is already defeated.

The non-dualistic mind says:

Practitioners of non-war have escaped the dualistic realm in which victory is inseparably linked to defeat. This is also the realm in which there is no escape from mistakes, for a finite "right action" is the polarity of a finite "wrong action." With the mind of duality, the finite rights and wrongs can never be separated, thus a person can never have one without the other.

Practitioners of non-war, having awakened from the illusions of duality, keep their minds attuned to the realm of the Infinite in which there is only *right* action. They do not seek to be right compared to other people or any standard in the finite world. They seek the incomparable right of oneness with the Infinite.

Those skilled in *right* action never seek to defeat but to enlighten others. This frees up their creative powers from being consumed by the dualistic struggle, thus opening the floodgates of the Infinite in manifesting the abundant life that is incomparable because it is beyond finite gain and loss.

The dualistic mind says:

Thus it is that in war the victorious strategist only seeks battle after the victory has been won, whereas he who is destined to defeat first fights and afterwards looks for victory.

The non-dualistic mind says:

Practitioners of non-war, being awakened from the illusions of duality, seek no finite victory and thus cannot suffer a finite defeat. They seek the incomparable victory that can come only from oneness with the Infinite.

The dualistic mind says:

The consummate leader cultivates the moral law, and strictly adheres to method and discipline; thus it is in his power to control success.

The non-dualistic mind says:

The truly consummate leaders free their minds from the illusions of duality, thereby rising above the finite moral law that is based on duality. Such leaders then find the superior moral law that is based on the reality of the Infinite and can be known only through union with the Infinite.

Such awakened leaders learn a superior method and discipline, thereby attaining an incomparable power to control success, the incomparable success that comes only from oneness with the Infinite.

Chapter 5.
Energy from the Infinite

The dualistic mind says:

The control of a large force is the same principle as the control of a few men: it is merely a question of dividing up their numbers.

The non-dualistic mind says:

The dualistic mind does not understand the true power of mind. Whenever two or more people are together in any endeavor, their minds combine to form a collective mind. The strength of the collective mind multiplies exponentially with the number of people.

When people who are trapped in duality come together, the power of their collective mind is far less than when awakened people come together. Thus, even a few awakened people can form a collective mind that is superior in strength to the collective mind of those in duality.

This is the only realistic hope for ending the age of war and bringing about a new age of abundance and peace. It is not realistic to hope that all people will become awakened within the near future. Yet if a critical mass of people will become awakened and come together in unity of vision and purpose, they can raise the collective mind beyond the illusions that lead to war.

One awakened being can have a major impact on raising the collective consciousness. Yet one person – no matter the level of enlightenment – cannot pull an entire planet beyond war, for that would be against free will.

The law of free will does not require that all people on Earth abandon the consciousness of war before there can be peace. It is sufficient that a critical mass of people abandon the consciousness of war, for then – although the collective consciousness is not completely pure – it will be impossible for war to break through to the physical realm.

The awakening of a critical mass of people from the illusions of duality is the *only* factor that can end the age of war and usher in the Golden Age of peace. This must be done by someone starting the process of removing the illusions of war from their own minds. These forerunners are the practitioners of non-war.

The dualistic mind says:

Indirect tactics, efficiently applied, are inexhaustible as Heaven and Earth, unending as the flow of rivers and streams; like the sun and moon, they end but to begin anew; like the four seasons, they pass away to return once more.

The non-dualistic mind says:

Having become blinded by illusions, the dualistic mind fails to see that nothing in the finite world is inexhaustible. For even Heaven and Earth will pass away, and only the Word of the Infinite shall not pass away.

Yet it is true that lifetimes can be spent on learning how to use finite tactics to defeat a finite enemy. A self-aware being has free will and thus has the right to engage in such pursuits for a long period of time. Yet eventually, those who continue the pursuit of finite excellence – even for what they deem to be a good cause – will exhaust their opportunity. No permanent profit or survival can be attained from finite appearances.

The practitioners of non-war, having been awakened from the illusions of duality, clearly see the futility of turning a finite endeavor into an end in itself. They know there is only one truly inexhaustible source of wisdom and energy, namely the Infinite. Only when the Infinite is brought into one's finite endeavors, will incomparable excellence be achieved.

While the sun of the Infinite shines upon the evil and the good and the energy of the Infinite rains upon the just and the unjust, only those who rise above duality can freely receive what is freely given. For only those above duality will not seek to hold on to the gifts of the Infinite. They will freely give – for the growth of the All – what they have freely received, thereby remaining in the River of Life.

The dualistic mind says:

There are not more than five musical notes, yet the combinations of these five give rise to more melodies than can ever be heard.

There are not more than five primary colors (blue, yellow, red, white, and black), yet in combination they produce more hues than can ever be seen.

There are not more than five cardinal tastes (sour, acrid, salt, sweet, bitter), yet combinations of them yield more flavors than can ever be tasted.

In battle, there are not more than two methods of attack—the direct and the indirect; yet these two in combination give rise to an endless series of maneuvers.

The non-dualistic mind says:

All self-aware beings have been given free will, so they have a right to pursue – for their allotted time – the seemingly endless combination of experiences that can be had through the five senses of the physical body.

The practitioners of non-war have had enough of this pursuit and desire something more. They have seen that duality is vanity and in the realm of duality, all is vanity. They know there is something beyond the finite world, and they want it more than they want anything in the finite world.

The dualistic mind says:

The direct and the indirect lead on to each other in turn. It is like moving in a circle—you never come to an end. Who can exhaust the possibilities of their combination?

The non-dualistic mind says:

Practitioners of non-war, having escaped the illusion of separation, know that anything in the finite world will have an end. They also know that it is possible to be so blinded by the illusions of duality that one does not realize that even though one is going around in a circle that seems to have no beginning or end, one's opportunity to walk this path did have a – distant – beginning and must have a – perhaps not so distant – end.

The practitioners of non-war desire more than this inconsequential pursuit of finite pleasure and gain. They know that for them to escape the finite merry-go-round – for them to escape the circle of the serpent swallowing its own tail – they must be willing to overcome the illusion of a separate self. For the separate self will never tire of pursuing finite experiences.

They must be willing to let the separate self die and be reborn into a higher sense of self. For they who seek to save the finite self will lose their lives, whereas those who are willing to lose the finite self – for the sake of following the path to the Infinite – will find eternal life.

The dualistic mind says:

The onset of troops is like the rush of a torrent which will even roll stones along in its course.

The non-dualistic mind says:

The practitioners of non-war understand the value of momentum. They see clearly that for eons the collective consciousness has been inundated by the dualistic mental images and the self-centered emotional energies generated by those trapped in duality. This has created a torrent that has attained considerable momentum.

The practitioners of non-war know that no individual and no small group of people can withstand the force of the torrent of the collective consciousness. Any attempt to engage or combat this consciousness will only cause one to be swept into the torrent, where one is driven with the wind and tossed.

Thus, with men it is impossible to stop the downward momentum of the collective consciousness, but with the Infinite all things are possible. Yet because of free will, the wisdom and power of the Infinite can work on Earth only when it is allowed to flow through those in embodiment, those who make themselves the open doors that no "man" – including their separate selves – can shut.

Practitioners of non-war do not seek excellence in finite pursuits and do not seek to build a finite momentum. They seek to become open doors for the infinite River of Life than can transform the muddied energies of the collective, dualistic consciousness back into their original crystal clarity, thus allowing people caught in the maelstrom to again see beyond the veil of finite energies.

Practitioners of non-war know that in order to serve as the open doors for the Infinite, they *must* stay out of the maelstrom of the collective consciousness. They must be vigilant in never responding to any situation in a dualistic manner. They must perform right action while remaining non-attached to the fruits of action.

In demonstrating this willingness to always reach beyond duality, they will build a momentum that will eventually reach critical mass and thus turn back the tides of war, allowing humanity to find rest on the shore of incomparable peace.

Yet before this can happen, the practitioners of non-war must be willing to stand fast against the torrents of war that will seek to tempt them, sweep them away or destroy their vision and resolve. This requires constant vigilance, for only those who have built their houses on the rock of the Infinite will be able to withstand the winds and rains of duality, that will surely try the work of every person who resists the momentum of duality.

For as like attracts like and misery wants company, the torrent of duality will resist those who refuse to be swept along by its planetary momentum. The key then is to be non-attached to finite conditions, so that the prince of duality will come and have nothing in you.

Yet beyond this, it is also necessary to use appropriate techniques for invoking the energy of the Infinite. Practitioners of non-war know that by unleashing the energies of the Infinite, they can serve to build a momentum that will sweep away the forces of war, washing the collective mind clean in the River of Life.

The dualistic mind says:

Energy may be likened to the bending of a crossbow; decision, to the releasing of a trigger.

The non-dualistic mind says:

The dualistic mind can only make use of the energies of the finite world. Thus, for it to accumulate energy to strike at the enemy, tension must be created. The energy that can be released toward the enemy is equal to the tension one generates, and generating tension depletes one of strength. The more tension that is generated, the more one's energy is depleted.

There is a limit to the destructive power that can be attained by any finite army, and thus such an army – no matter the power it commands – can never escape the possibility of defeat.

No decision made by the dualistic mind can release more energy than the tension generated by that mind. No army engaged in a dualistic struggle can ever be certain of defeating the enemy. One's own destruction is always a possibility.

Practitioners of non-war are not seeking to destroy the enemy, thus have no need to generate finite tension and make dualistic decisions. Instead, they draw upon the inexhaustible energy of the Infinite, an energy that is not created and thus needs no tension. Using this energy will not deplete one's strength, but will increase it. The more infinite energy one allows to flow through one's energy field, the more one's strength will be increased.

There is no limit to the constructive power that can be released through the unified minds of those who have awakened from duality and vowed to be the open doors for the Infinite. They are above the possibility of defeat, for the Infinite knows only unopposed Victory.

Practitioners of non-war have no need to make decisions with the dualistic mind. Their decisions need not be calculated or based on thought systems and rules in the finite world. Instead, they spring spontaneously from the mind that is attuned to the incomparable wisdom of the Infinite. Such non-dualistic decisions can release an energy that can transform any finite condition and bring it closer to infinity. With the Infinite, truly all things are possible.

Practitioners of non-war know that in order to set themselves free from the downward pull of duality, they must use proper techniques for invoking energy directly from the Infinite. Likewise, in order to set other people free – even set an entire planet free – the energies of duality must be transmuted through the invocation of energy from the Infinite.

The low-frequency energy produced through the filter of duality must be transformed through interaction with the high-frequency energy from the Infinite. Becoming open doors for this incomparable energy is a primary goal for practitioners of non-war.

The dualistic mind says:

Simulated disorder postulates perfect discipline, simulated fear postulates courage; simulated weakness postulates strength.

   Hiding order beneath the cloak of disorder is simply a question of subdivision; concealing courage under a show of timidity presupposes a fund of latent energy; masking strength with weakness is to be effected by tactical dispositions.

The non-dualistic mind says:

Fortunate are those who have risen above the need to deceive, for their minds are free to draw on the inexhaustible supply of the Infinite, causing them to manifest the truly abundant life instead of being consumed by the dualistic struggle.

The dualistic mind says:

Hiding order beneath the cloak of disorder is simply a question of subdivision.

The non-dualistic mind says:

One cannot divide the enemy without dividing oneself. Once divided, one will inevitably be blinded by the illusions of duality, whereby one is cut off from the incomparable abundance of the Infinite. This is not true wisdom, not real advantage and not eternal life.

When seeking to deceive another, two people will be deceived. When seeking to subdue another, two people will be subdued by the ongoing struggle. When seeking to destroy another, two people will be swept along by the momentum of destruction.

The dualistic mind says:

Thus the energy developed by good fighting men is as the momentum of a round stone rolled down a mountain thousands of feet in height. So much on the subject of energy.

The non-dualistic mind says:

The energy released by a stone rolling down a mountain is the same that is required to push the stone up the mountain. It is finite and when the stone reaches the bottom of the slope, nothing is left.

In pursuing selfish goals that do not enhance the All, practitioners of war confine themselves to the energy available in the material realm. This energy is finite, thus the ability to wage war is finite. One can gather energy temporarily and perhaps even conquer empires on Earth. But once the energy is spent, there is nothing left and one is depleted.

Practitioners of non-war have raised themselves above selfish pursuits and are working to raise the All. Thus, they have access to the stream of energy that flows from the Infinite into the finite world for the purpose of bringing the finite closer to the Infinite. This energy can never be exhausted.

Practitioners of non-war will never be depleted, for as they multiply their talents by doing for others what they want others to do for them, they are given more than they spend.

The more energy spent by a practitioner of war, the less is left, for the supply is finite. The more energy spent by a practitioner of non-war, the more is received, for the supply is infinite.

Chapter 6.
Beyond Strong and Weak Points

The dualistic mind says:

Whoever is first in the field and awaits the coming of the enemy, will be fresh for the fight; whoever is second in the field and has to hasten to battle will arrive exhausted.

The non-dualistic mind says:

Practitioners of war are trapped in the dualistic mind and see themselves as being boxed in by limitations. Yet they fail to see that those limitations are created by themselves because they have projected dualistic mental images into the cosmic mirror.

One of the seemingly most insurmountable limitations created by the dualistic mind is time. Yet only a mind separated from the Infinite can believe that the flow of life can be divided into past, present and future. For when one sees that there can be no divisions in the Infinite, how can one believe the flow of life can be divided into separate compartments?

Practitioners of non-war seek first the kingdom of the Infinite and its righteousness—the right use of one's creative faculties. They immerse themselves in the River of Life and know that there is no impenetrable barrier between past, present and future. This is eternal life.

There is only one time, namely the Eternal NOW. When one is in the Eternal NOW, one can transform one's past and master one's future. Thus, there is no need for haste, no need to feel that one is behind. For when one is in the Eternal NOW, for what purpose would one need to hurry to catch up? And compared to what point could one fall behind?

All will happen at the right time, and if something does not happen, then one remains at peace in knowing that in the River of Life everything is on time. One can thus let tomorrow take care of itself and appreciate the incomparable beauty of the present moment. When expectations about what should or should not happen – and *when* it should or should not happen – are left behind, where is the room for disappointment?

Practitioners of war are driven by time as a ship without rudder is driven by the wind. They might be behind, they might be ahead, but they are rarely in the NOW. Practitioners of non-war, having awakened from the illusions of duality, know that finite time is not, for only the River of Life is real. Thus, they live in the Eternal NOW in which time is as indivisible as the Infinite.

The dualistic mind says:

Therefore the clever combatant imposes his will on the enemy, but does not allow the enemy's will to be imposed on him.

The non-dualistic mind says:

In seeking to force a selfish will upon a self-created enemy, one must first force a selfish will upon oneself.

Thus, one will inevitably become imprisoned by that selfish will, which cannot be the will of one's infinite Being. One therefore becomes a slave of a selfish will, be it the will of one's own ego or an external force.

Practitioners of war spend their lives seeking to force the selfish will upon others without ever seeing that they have first imprisoned themselves in a cage that is smaller than the cage in which they are seeking to trap others.

Practitioners of non-war attune their minds to the one will of the Infinite, individualized in the will of their infinite selves. They know that this does not make them marionettes, for the will of the Infinite merely forms a framework. Within it, there is infinite room for individual expression.

The will of the Infinite is like the force of gravity. While gravity may seem to restrict one's movements on Earth, without it there would be no Earth upon which to move. Is it wise to spend one's life rebelling against the law of gravity and attempting to pull oneself up by one's own bootstraps? Or is it better to learn how to use all of the laws of nature, including learning how to use other laws to partially suspend gravity and fly through the air?

Practitioners of war always feel as if someone – on Earth or in Heaven – is seeking to force an exterior will upon them. Practitioners of non-war know they are extensions of the Infinite, and thus the will of the Infinite is not an external will. It is the framework in which they can safely exercise their individual will in such a way that any decision they make leads to the growth of the All—which includes themselves.

The dualistic mind says:

An army may march great distances without distress, if it marches through country where the enemy is not.

The non-dualistic mind says:

Practitioners of non-war may move indefinitely without distress, for they march with a mind that creates no enemies and thus produces no resistance to its movement.

The dualistic mind says:

You can be sure of succeeding in your attacks if you only attack places which are undefended. You can ensure the safety of your defense if you only hold positions that cannot be attacked.

The non-dualistic mind says:

The only way to be truly sure of succeeding is to never attack and never defend but to rise above the duality of attack and defense. When the mind is free of the dualistic opposites, one will attain a state of incomparable success.

For when the image one projects into the cosmic mirror has no internal contradictions, how can the mirror reflect back anything but the indivisible abundance of the Infinite?

The dualistic mind says:

O divine art of subtlety and secrecy! Through you we learn to be invisible, through you inaudible; and hence we can hold the enemy's fate in our hands.

The non-dualistic mind says:

The truly divine art is one of union with the reality of the Infinite in which nothing is hidden. Thus, there is no need – indeed no room – for subtlety and secrecy.

Practitioners of non-war, having risen above the dualistic illusions, see clearly how the dualistic mind works. They see that the dualistic mind uses its own internal contradictions to formulate a mental image, and then it projects that image upon everything.

Those trapped in the dualistic mind spend their lives seeking to defend their mental boxes—their graven images. They seek to force the entire universe to fit into their self-created thought system. The most arrogant of them even seek to force the Infinite to fit into their finite mental boxes.

Practitioners of non-war see clearly that no mental box created through the dualistic mind could ever contain even the material universe, let alone the Infinite. Thus, they spend their lives going beyond all mental boxes, seeking union with the Infinite instead of seeking to control that which cannot be controlled. They seek to expand their mental boxes to infinity rather than seeking to fit infinity into a finite box.

Practitioners of non-war see clearly that there can be no subtlety and secrecy in the Infinite, for it is indivisible. Only when there is separation, can there be division. Only when there is division, can anything be hidden. And only when something is hidden, can there be subtlety and secrecy.

Practitioners of war desire to hide from the Infinite, so they want a world in which divisions exist. Yet what you hide from others, you must first hide from yourself, so who is the first person to become blind?

Duality seems desirable to those who do not want to take full responsibility for themselves, for it allows them to create veils of illusion that they think are impenetrable to both men and the Infinite. Yet why is it that human beings continue to believe in the illusion that what they can hide from each other is also hidden from the Infinite?

The Infinite is All and in all, and thus it sees all. Practitioners of non-war have transcended the desire to hide from the Infinite. They have taken full responsibility for themselves and as such have nothing to hide. They give up their finite lives and seek the eternal life that comes only from oneness with the Infinite. In oneness there is no need for secrecy.

Practitioners of non-war see that people left paradise because they wanted to hide their dualistic nakedness from the Infinite. Practitioners of non-war have decided that they no longer want to hide from the Infinite, so they look at and remove the beam of duality in their own eyes. Hereby, they become the pure in heart, and thus they see the Infinite. Being pure, they can see the Infinite and live, for they no longer live as humans but as the spiritual beings they were created to be.

The dualistic mind says:

You may advance and be absolutely irresistible, if you make for the enemy's weak points; you may retire and be safe from pursuit if your movements are more rapid than those of the enemy.

The non-dualistic mind says:

Nothing in the finite world can be absolute, thus no finite army can ever be irresistible. Again, the dualistic mind creates illusions and then seeks to elevate them to the status of being the absolute truth. An illusion may be believed and affirmed by billions of people, yet it is still an illusion. The Earth was round even when most people believed it to be flat.

Practitioners of non-war do not seek to defend their illusions. They let the scales fall from their eyes. They know that the only way to be truly irresistible is through oneness with the Infinite, the only absolute that exists.

They also know that in order to be one with the Infinite, they must seek to raise up the All instead of seeking to raise the separate self. Instead of exploiting the weak points of other people, they seek to help them overcome their weak points. For it is in giving that you truly receive and in raising up others that you are raised.

The Infinite wants to raise up all self-aware beings. Only by working for this goal, can you join forces with the Infinite. Holding on to the illusion of separation – and the sense of competition or conflict with other people – can never lead to oneness with the One.

The dualistic mind says:

If we wish to fight, the enemy can be forced to an engagement even though he be sheltered behind a high rampart and a deep ditch. All we need do is attack some other place that he will be obliged to relieve.

The non-dualistic mind says:

In seeking to awaken others, it is necessary to acknowledge that people often defend their mental boxes and that they feel any challenge of a deeply held belief is an attack. Once people feel you are attacking, it is very difficult to open their minds to a higher understanding.

Practitioners of non-war know when to withdraw and seek to circumvent people's defenses in order to approach the issue from an unexpected direction that avoids the defensive response. This, of course, is not done to manipulate people's will but to enlighten them to the advantage of leaving their mental boxes and opening their minds to the incomparable wisdom of the Infinite.

The dualistic mind says:

If we do not wish to fight, we can prevent the enemy from engaging us even though the lines of our encampment be merely traced out on the ground. All we need do is to throw something odd and unaccountable in his way.

The non-dualistic mind says:

Practitioners of non-war never want to fight and are always seeking to avoid having other people go into a defensive reaction. Once people have circled their wagons and built fortifications against the advance of your ideas, nothing good can be achieved by pressing the issue further.

Practitioners of non-war seek to avoid this reaction by presenting ideas that surprise others, making them think without directly threatening their most deeply held beliefs.

Practitioners of non-war know that you will rarely awaken people through a frontal attack on their mental box. The reason is that people derive a sense of security from their mental boxes, and thus attaching the box makes people feel insecure and threatened. The instinctive response is to defend their mental boxes by closing their minds. Some will even seek to destroy your ideas—or yourself.

If one can surprise people with an unexpected and unaccountable idea, one can potentially cause them to think without feeling that their security is threatened. This might help people see that there is greater security or greater abundance to be found by expanding one's mental box rather than defending it.

This can gradually lead people to realize that ultimate security can never be found in any finite belief system but only through union with the Infinite. It is never constructive to seek to break down people's resistance by saying their present beliefs are wrong. It is far better to present them with the advantage of expanding their beliefs.

If you attack and seek to break down people's mental boxes, they will only seek to defend them. If you seek to help people expand their mental boxes, soon their old boxes will be forgotten. They will be dissolved without people feeling threatened.

Practitioners of non-war know that one cannot force others to expand their understanding. Expanding one's mind must be a voluntary, creative process that comes from within.

Practitioners of non-war never seek to force others to accept certain ideas. They seek to help others internalize new ideas, so they choose to accept them because they see that it is in their own best interest.

Practitioners of war are trapped in pursuing their own self-interest, which they think necessitates using force against those who define their self-interest differently. Practitioners of non-war have attained enlightened self-interest. They know this means helping other people see that true self-interest is to help all people unite with the Infinite. For by doing so, all will experience a life of incomparable abundance.

Practitioners of non-war are always seeking to awaken others to the incomparable advantage that comes from union with the Infinite.

The dualistic mind says:

By discovering the enemy's dispositions and remaining invisible ourselves, we can keep our forces concentrated, while the enemy's must be divided.

The non-dualistic mind says:

Practitioners of non-war have uncompromising respect for the free will and individuality of others. Thus, they do not approach an interaction with the attitude that they are superior—and therefore others should instantly agree with them. Instead, they keep their own viewpoints invisible while seeking to understand other people's frame of mind.

Only when understanding others do practitioners of non-war advance their ideas. For only then can they know how to present those ideas in such a way that other people do not feel threatened and go into a defensive position by closing their minds and hearts.

Practitioners of war seek to force others to accept their ideas, thinking their ideas are infallible. Practitioners of non-war are not attached to particular ideas. They seek to open the minds of others to a higher understanding.

Practitioners of non-war seek to give each person what he or she needs in order to take the next step toward the Infinite. They are focused on helping living people, not on advancing dead ideas.

The dualistic mind says:

We can form a single united body, while the enemy must split up into fractions. Hence there will be a whole pitted against separate parts of a whole, which means that we shall be many to the enemy's few.

The non-dualistic mind says:

Practitioners of non-war do not seek to divide the enemy. They seek first unity with the Infinite and then they seek unity with others. They know that only when all members have established their individual connections to the Infinite, can there be a truly united body.

In some cases it is appropriate to point out the divisions in the minds of others in the form of contradictions or inconsistencies in their viewpoints. Such contradictions are abundant in the minds of those who are blinded by dualistic illusions.

Yet in pointing out flaws in the reasoning of other people, practitioners of non-war never seek to prove others wrong or themselves superior. They only seek to awaken others to the incomparable advantage of coming into unity with the Infinite.

The dualistic mind says:

Numerical weakness comes from having to prepare against possible attacks; numerical strength, from compelling our adversary to make these preparations against us.

The non-dualistic mind says:

Numerical advantage is a finite advantage, and it is not sought by practitioners of non-war. They do not allow themselves to feel attacked, and they seek to prevent others from feeling attacked.

They seek to help others escape the "fog of war" represented by the duality consciousness, rather than seeking to force people into becoming even more blinded by illusions.

Practitioners of non-war do not seek any finite advantage. They know that any finite number can be exceeded by a larger number, and thus one can spend one's allotted time chasing the ultimate finite advantage without ever achieving it.

Practitioners of non-war seek the incomparable advantage of union with the Infinite. They know that in the indivisible reality of the Infinite, One is always a majority.

The dualistic mind says:

How victory may be produced for them out of the enemy's own tactics—that is what the multitude cannot comprehend.

The non-dualistic mind says:

When you understand the minds of others, you see how to help them overcome the dualistic inconsistencies that will inevitably be found in their thinking. For there can be no dualistic viewpoint that is not inseparably linked to its opposite, and thus all dualistic beliefs have inconsistencies and contradictions.

Practitioners of war will use such inconsistencies to defeat their enemies. Practitioners of non-war use them to awaken others.

Do not use inconsistencies to prove others wrong or to destroy their beliefs. Point out inconsistencies and then show people how they can be resolved by adopting a non-dualistic understanding of the issue.

Practitioners of non-war know that every inconsistency that springs from the mind of duality can be overcome by understanding the topic through the wisdom of the Infinite. Thus, there is no problem that does not have a solution.

However, solutions can be found only by those who recognize that all problems spring from the dualistic mind and that solutions can be found only by transcending that mind. For one cannot solve a problem with the same state of consciousness that created the problem.

Not even the cleverest person can remove darkness from a room. Darkness has no reality, and thus it can be overcome only by bringing that which has reality, namely the incomparable Light of the Infinite.

Practitioners of non-war see the subtle reality that people became divided within themselves because they did not understand that in the dualistic mind – in the realm of relative good and relative evil – any idea will have an opposing idea. Thus, when exposed to the opposing idea, people's minds were divided by the arrows of doubt, causing them to wonder which of the two opposing ideas might be true.

Practitioners of non-war see that the only antidote to the poison of doubt is to reconnect to the incomparable wisdom of the Infinite. Thereby, one will gain an understanding that goes beyond the opposing ideas, seeing that both of the opposing ideas are out of touch with the indivisible reality of the infinite.

The dualistic mind says:

Do not repeat the tactics which have gained you one victory, but let your methods be regulated by the infinite variety of circumstances.

The non-dualistic mind says:

People blinded by the dualistic mind have come to accept certain mental images. They refuse to expand them, whereby they become graven images that obscure the ever-moving River of Life. Thus, they will often be blinded by the insanity that causes people to keep doing the same thing while expecting different results.

Practitioners of non-war realize that every person is an individual, and thus one must never fall prey to the temptation to generalize. Approach every situation and every person as unique, for in doing so you give room for the Infinite to enter.

If, on the other hand, you think one situation should be handled as a previous situation, you are saying that you can do it yourself and that you don't need the Infinite. This is not the way of the practitioners of non-war.

They realize the truth that they can of their own selves do nothing; it is the Infinite within them who is doing the work. Thus, they give room for the Infinite to enter every situation.

Practitioners of non-war do not passively wait for the Infinite to do all the work for them. For they know that the Infinite can help only those who help themselves by taking responsibility for multiplying their talents. They understand the need to find balance by avoiding the dualistic extremes of thinking one can do nothing or can do everything.

Practitioners of non-war seek the middle way, whereby the Infinite works hitherto and they work.

The dualistic mind says:

Military tactics are like unto water; for water in its natural course runs away from high places and hastens downwards.

The non-dualistic mind says:

Practitioners of war may think they are seeking the path of least resistance. Yet because they are trapped in the dualistic mind, they can never escape the resistance that is created by themselves. For every dualistic illusion creates resistance through its internal contradictions.

Practitioners of non-war do not seek the path of least resistance but seek the true path of non-resistance that comes from rising above duality. They do not seek the low places but always reach for the high place of the Infinite.

The dualistic mind says:

So in war, the way is to avoid what is strong and to strike at what is weak.

The non-dualistic mind says:

Practitioners of non-war seek to increase what is strong and raise up what is weak. They never seek to break down but only to build up. For they know that when they send out the signal that they want to build up others, the cosmic mirror must inevitably reflect back material circumstances that build up themselves.

Practitioners of war believe in the dualistic illusion of lack and scarcity. Thus, it follows that for some to win, others must lose. For some to be the "haves," others must be the "have-nots."

Practitioners of non-war see that by tapping the inexhaustible wisdom and energy of the Infinite, lack and scarcity can be transcended. Thus, it is entirely possible to create material circumstances in which all people have the abundant life and thus all are winners.

Why fight over what is available in abundance? Why seek to take from others what is given freely to all who will receive it?

The dualistic mind says:

Water shapes its course according to the nature of the ground over which it flows; the soldier works out his victory in relation to the foe whom he is facing.

The non-dualistic mind says:

Practitioners of non-war adapt their interactions with others to these people's state of mind so as to better help them grow. Yet in their own minds, they always follow the course toward union with the Infinite, letting no finite conditions distract them from this goal.

112

The dualistic mind says:

Therefore, just as water retains no constant shape, so in warfare there are no constant conditions.

The non-dualistic mind says:

Practitioners of non-war recognize that there are no constant conditions in the finite world, and thus they approach every situation as unique. Yet they also see beyond the finite world and find incomparable constancy in the Infinite.

The dualistic mind says:

He who can modify his tactics in relation to his opponent and thereby succeed in winning, may be called a heaven-born captain.

The non-dualistic mind says:

They who can modify their tactics in order to help others come closer to the Infinite – while in their own selves remaining steadfast in union with the Infinite – can truly succeed and are truly heaven-born.

The dualistic mind says:

The five elements (water, fire, wood, metal, earth) are not always equally predominant; the four seasons make way for each other in turn. There are short days and long; the moon has its periods of waning and waxing.

The non-dualistic mind says:

Practitioners of non-war understand that there are cycles in the finite world, and thus one must give other people time to grow in understanding. Often, a person needs to process new ideas in the higher levels of the mind before they can be accepted by the conscious mind. Thus, in one's patience one will possess one's soul and help others possess theirs.

The levels of the mind correspond to the levels of the world of form. This can be understood only by those who see that everything is made from energy and that energy vibrates at different levels.

As there is a division of light into infra-red, visible and ultra-violet, the energies that make up the world of form are divided into levels. Some of these levels of vibration cannot be detected by the senses or by current scientific instruments, but this does not make them any less real.

Practitioners of non-war do not scoff at that which is not seen by the senses or understood by science. They learn about the subtler energies and learn to use them in awakening others.

In seeking to awaken others, one must appeal to all levels of the mind. They are:

- **The conscious mind.** For many people this mind is attuned to the physical body and the material universe. Appeal to it by presenting people with a concrete advantage for expanding their minds. Know their minds and present them with an advantage – such as greater abundance – that they can grasp in their current state of consciousness. Then gradually help them see a greater advantage, until they grasp the incomparable advantage of union with the Infinite.

- **The emotional mind.** This is the seat of people's creative drive. Fear and other negative emotions paralyze people, whereas positive emotions set energy in motion. To move people out of the inertia of wanting everything to stay the same, understand that the emotions are always seeking security. The ultimate goal of the emotional mind is peace. Help people see that ultimate peace can never be attained through finite means but can be attained only through union with the Infinite.

- **The mental mind.** At the level of thoughts, people seek to understand. People trapped in duality seek to understand the finite world and use that understanding to gain a finite advantage compared to others. This is because the analytical mind does not understand moral or ethical considerations. It is a relative mind that sees no ultimate right or wrong but only what seems to give a temporary advantage.

  Yet the thinking mind is capable of seeing the inconsistencies in dualistic ideas. Appeal to it by helping people find a greater understanding, which is the goal of the thinking mind. Then gradually help them see that ultimate wisdom cannot be attained in the finite world but only through union with the Infinite.

- **The identity mind.** This is the highest level of the lower mind, and it is the meeting point, the doorway, between the lower mind and the spiritual self. It contains the identity through which you express your creative powers in the material world. It forms a filter through which you see everything. If the identity mind contains a true identity – namely that you are an expression of the Infinite – you can draw on the wisdom and energy of the Infinite. If the identity mind contains a separate sense of identity – a separate, mortal self – you cannot draw upon any wisdom and energy from beyond the finite world. Thus, your creative powers will be limited and your decisions must be based on finite wisdom.

These are the four levels of the lower mind, also called the container of self or the soul. Yet complete self-knowledge includes knowing the higher levels of the mind:

- **The conscious self.** This is where self-awareness – and thus free will – is centered. The conscious self is an extension of the Infinite and as such can be aware of both the lower mind and the spiritual self. It is only the conscious self that can receive the non-dualistic wisdom of the Infinite. Yet this can only happen when the conscious self accepts itself as an extension of the Infinite. If the conscious self has become blinded by the illusions of duality – seeing itself as a sinner, as a mortal human being or as a highly evolved animal – it will think it has a right to do anything it wants. Thus, it cannot grasp the non-dualistic reality of the Infinite, which is the *only* possible basis for unselfish morality and ethics.

The conscious self has an eternal longing for union with something greater than itself, a longing that people can silence but only for a time. One can appeal to this longing and help people see that its ultimate fulfillment can be achieved only through complete union with the Infinite. This does not mean the loss of individuality but the elevation of individuality from a finite unreality to an infinite reality.

It is the conscious self that can choose to accept the illusion of separation and thus become blinded by the veil of duality. Yet because the conscious self is an extension of the Infinite, it can never lose its ability to awaken from the illusion of separation and reunite with the Infinite. The conscious self is meant to keep the lower mind in alignment with the spiritual self and make conscious decisions based on the divine plan anchored in the spiritual self. If the conscious self refuses to fulfill this role, and becomes blinded by the illusion of separation, a separate self – the ego – is created. This separate self will then make most decisions. Since it is born from separation, the ego can only make decisions based on the dualistic mind. The ego can never use the wisdom of the Infinite to make decisions that lead to the growth of the All.

- **The spiritual self.** This is a level of the mind that is above and beyond anything in the finite world. It cannot be affected by any mistake a person has made in this world, meaning that no matter what mistakes one has made, the spiritual self is still pure. This is what gives all people the possibility of escaping all finite mistakes and once again rising to their proper status as pure extensions of the Infinite. The spiritual self is the storehouse of one's infinite individuality and of all right decisions made during one's journey in the finite world. It is one's treasure laid up in Heaven, and the wise ones learn to draw upon this cosmic bank account in order to make wise investments. The admonishment, "Man, know thyself," truly means, "Human, know thy infinite Self."

When you have self-knowledge, there will be an unrestricted flow of wisdom and energy from your infinite self into your lower being, where it is directed by your conscious self. Any unselfish act will close the circle, so the energies can flow back up to the spiritual self, where they are multiplied and sent back. This sacred figure-eight flow is the key to the abundant life.

Practitioners of non-war seek to know the subtler levels of their own minds. When they achieve this knowledge, they use it to help other people know their own minds. They also see how to appeal to all levels of a person's mind, allowing an idea to cycle through from the identity to the mental, to the emotional, to the conscious mind.

Practitioners of non-war never seek to force people into accepting their ideas here and now. They are content to spread ideas as one would sow seeds. And they are content to let their seed ideas be buried in the ground – meaning the subconscious levels of the mind – for a time before they break through the surface and are acceptable to a person's conscious mind.

Those who work for tomorrow plant trees. Those who work for eternity plant ideas.

Chapter 7.
Non-dualistic Maneuvering

The dualistic mind says:

In war, the general receives his commands from the sovereign.

The non-dualistic mind says:

The "general" is a symbol for those who have made it their calling and craft to fight a finite war against a finite enemy. Many professional warriors will fight any battle their sovereign commands them to fight, for without the sovereign they could not exist. In doing so, they have suspended their responsibility to make moral and ethical judgments and have made themselves the blind followers of whomever they have accepted as their finite sovereign.

Practitioners of non-war accept no finite leader as their sovereign. They accept only one sovereign, namely the Infinite. Thus, they accept their moral and ethical responsibility to never follow any finite leader blindly.

This does not mean that practitioners of non-war accept no finite leaders, for any society must have leaders. But they accept only leaders who have the incomparable moral law of the Infinite. Thus, they refuse to – in any way – perpetuate or take part in dualistic conflicts.

Practitioners of war believe blind obedience to a leader is a virtue and that following a leader relieves them of moral responsibility for their actions. This is a failure to accept responsibility for oneself, and it can only lead to further separation from the Infinite.

Practitioners of non-war accept responsibility for themselves and accept that people are never free from moral responsibility. One is not being moral in blindly following a leader, for if the leader has abandoned the moral law of the Infinite, one cannot avoid violating this law. Those following a leader are still sending impulses into the cosmic mirror, and the mirror can only reflect back what is sent out.

Practitioners of non-war know that it is their moral responsibility to – in non-violent and non-deceitful ways – speak out against a leader who has abandoned the true moral law and has engaged in a dualistic conflict. By doing so one might not receive any reward on Earth, but one is sure to receive an incomparable reward in the realm of the Infinite.

The dualistic mind says:

To take a long and circuitous route, after enticing the enemy out of the way, and though starting after him, to contrive to reach the goal before him, shows knowledge of the artifice of deviation.

The non-dualistic mind says:

Deviating from a norm or standard practice is wise, but to the dualistic mind this merely means finding another tactic that also springs from the mind of duality yet is not known or mastered by the enemy.

Practitioners of non-war are seeking to deviate from the illusions of the dualistic mind that have been elevated to the standard of infallible doctrines. Thus, they practice the higher form of deviation.

When practitioners of war practice finite deviation, they only bring themselves further into the jungle of dualistic illusions. When practitioners of non-war practice non-dual deviation, they raise themselves above the jungle and breathe the clear, cool air of the Infinite. They see the farthest horizons that are invisible and undreamt of to those fighting their way through the jungle.

The dualistic mind says:

We may take it then that an army without its baggage-train is lost; without provisions it is lost; without bases of supply it is lost.

The non-dualistic mind says:

Practitioners of war seek a baggage train and provisions in the finite world. Practitioners of non-war look to the Infinite as the only true source of everything they need. They know that when they seek first oneness with the Infinite, all finite things – that they truly need – will be added unto them.

Practitioners of non-war accept that if they do not have it, it is because they do not need it. Thus, they avoid the subtle trap of the illusion of lack, which causes people to feel that they are deprived of something in the finite world. Practitioners of non-war avoid sending images of lack into the cosmic mirror and they avoid the illusion that their wholeness depends on anything in the finite world.

They fully accept that the kingdom of the Infinite is within them and that the Infinite is the source of all good and perfect things.

The dualistic mind says:

We cannot enter into alliances until we are acquainted with the designs of our neighbors.

The non-dualistic mind says:

One cannot enter into a true alliance until one has pulled the beam of duality from one's own eye and has helped one's neighbor do the same. True alliances are not based on dualistic self-interest but on enlightened self-interest that seeks to raise up the All.

Only when all members have attained their individual connections to the Infinite, can there be a true alliance. This is an alliance that cannot be broken by the many subtle temptations of the dualistic mind that always seeks to divide that it may conquer. An alliance that is based on oneness with the Infinite cannot be divided by finite means.

The dualistic mind says:

We are not fit to lead an army on the march unless we are familiar with the face of the country—its mountains and forests, its pitfalls and precipices, its marshes and swamps.

The non-dualistic mind says:

Practitioners of non-war also study the terrain, meaning that they seek to learn how the material world currently works. Yet they do this only for the purpose of seeing how material conditions can be used to bring forth the abundant life for all.

Practitioners of non-war are open to the reality that by drawing on the wisdom and energy of the Infinite, even material conditions can be transformed and improved. For it is indeed possible to return planet Earth to its former purity, when the abundant life was manifest for all.

When a critical mass of human beings are awakened, it will even be possible to go beyond the original state of abundance to manifest a Golden Age that is beyond what most people – blinded by the illusions of scarcity and lack – can even dream about.

Practitioners of non-war dare to dream the non-dualistic dreams of the Infinite. For they have awakened themselves from the dualistic nightmare in which most people are trapped.

The dualistic mind says:

We shall be unable to turn natural advantage to account unless we make use of local guides.

The non-dualistic mind says:

Naturally, practitioners of non-war consult those who have greater expertise in certain fields than themselves.

Yet in listening to such advice, they are aware that it must be put in its proper context.

A person may be a great expert in a finite field of knowledge, but if the person is not awakened to the reality of the Infinite, he or she will often see material conditions as unchangeable.

Practitioners of non-war never accept any finite conditions as unchangeable, for they know that with the wisdom and energy of the Infinite, all things are possible. They know that the formless energy that makes up the Earth can as easily manifest the abundant life as it can manifest the current state of limitations and suffering.

The dualistic mind says:

In war, practice dissimulation, and you will succeed.

The non-dualistic mind says:

By disguising their intentions and thoughts, practitioners of war bind themselves to the illusions of the dualistic mind. For only in the mind that is separated from the Infinite is it possible to practice deceit.

Practitioners of non-war are ever vigilant that they do not practice finite dissimulation but always retain their tie to the Infinite. This can be done only by following the timeless admonishment to be true to one's own – infinite – self.

One can withhold one's ideas until one knows how to present them to others, but one is never deceitful or manipulative. For before one can be dishonest with others, open must first be dishonest with oneself, and this will separate one from the Infinite in which no dishonesty is possible.

The dualistic mind says:

When you plunder a countryside, let the spoil be divided amongst your men; when you capture new territory, cut it up into allotments for the benefit of the soldiery.

The non-dualistic mind says:

Make sure that any advantage that is achieved as the result of cooperation with others is made to benefit all participants in a just and fair manner, where each is rewarded according to his or her contribution.

Let people's reward be based on their own multiplication of their talents—not according to the amount of their talents.

The dualistic mind says:

Ponder and deliberate before you make a move.

The non-dualistic mind says:

Attune to the Infinite before you make a move. Finite deliberations will get you nowhere closer to incomparable Victory.

The dualistic mind says:

Gongs and drums, banners and flags, are means whereby the ears and eyes of the host may be focused on one particular point.
The host thus forming a single united body, it is impossible either for the brave to advance alone, or for the cowardly to retreat alone. This is the art of handling large masses of men.

The non-dualistic mind says:

The true way to handle large groups is to make sure their minds are focused on a single point by awakening them to the reality of the Infinite. Once united in a common vision, people can move toward victory independently without being controlled from a central point in the finite world.

Practitioners of non-war are united through the central point of the Infinite and their vision of enlightened self-interest. This is how to form a truly united body, a body that cannot be divided by dualistic illusions and thus cannot be conquered by any finite force.

The dualistic mind says:

A whole army may be robbed of its spirit; a commander-in-chief may be robbed of his presence of mind.

The non-dualistic mind says:

Those who have built their house on the rock of the Infinite can never lose their spirit, for only a finite spirit can be lost. A commander who is attuned to the incomparable wisdom of the Infinite can never lose presence of mind.

The dualistic mind says:

Disciplined and calm, to await the appearance of disorder and hubbub amongst the enemy: this is the art of retaining self-possession.

The non-dualistic mind says:

True self-possession can be attained only through union with the Infinite. This is a self-possession that is independent of other people or finite conditions. It is so because it is based on union with the Self that is beyond the finite world.

This does not mean that a person has attained some ultimate state of control—which is what practitioners of war seek. It means that the person has surrendered all attachments to finite conditions and is now possessed – owned – by the Infinite Self. This is SELF-possession that empowers practitioners of non-war to say, "I and my infinite Self are one."

The dualistic mind says:

To be near the goal while the enemy is still far from it, to wait at ease while the enemy is toiling and struggling, to be well-fed while the enemy is famished: this is the art of husbanding one's strength.

The non-dualistic mind says:

To truly husband one's strength means making it independent of any finite conditions. Practitioners of non-war base their strength on union with the Infinite, which is the source of incomparable strength.

The dualistic mind says:

To refrain from intercepting an enemy whose banners are in perfect order, to refrain from attacking an army drawn up in calm and confident array: this is the art of studying circumstances.

The non-dualistic mind says:

To learn how to bring oneself into union with the Infinite and then use that knowledge to help others bring themselves into union with the Infinite—this is the incomparable art of studying circumstances. It leads practitioners of non-war to incomparable success.

Chapter 8.
Non-dual Variation in Tactics

The dualistic mind says:

In war, the general receives his commands from the sovereign, collects his army and concentrates his forces.

The non-dualistic mind says:

In non-war, all participants are united through their individual unity with the Infinite. Thus, none are sovereigns and none are blind followers. Though some take up leadership positions, others follow directions because they see them as enlightened self-interest.

The dualistic mind says:

Do not linger in dangerously isolated positions. In hemmed-in situations, you must resort to stratagem. In desperate positions, you must fight.

The non-dualistic mind says:

When you allow your mind to be controlled by the illusions of duality, you will be forced along by finite circumstances. You will often find yourself in desperate situations, where it seems like fighting is the only possible response. This is how the dualistic struggle has been sustained and perpetuated for so long on this planet—by people walking blindly into situations where it seems like the only way out is to fight.

Practitioners of non-war maintain their connection to the Infinite, so they avoid being pushed along by finite circumstances. However, they cannot avoid all undesirable situations, for they do not violate the free will of others.

Practitioners of non-war are never blinded by the illusions of duality. They never feel the desperation that makes it seem like fighting is the only way out. Instead, they often avoid tension and danger. And even when it cannot be avoided, they do not resort to fighting. They know that one always has an alternative to fighting, namely to turn the other cheek.

By fighting, one only binds oneself to the dualistic struggle. By turning the other cheek, one sets oneself free from the struggle and even helps to make it easier for other people to rise above the struggle.

When one knows that one is an extension of the Infinite, how could finite conditions ever cause one to feel desperation?

The dualistic mind says:

There are roads which must not be followed, armies which must be not attacked, towns which must not be besieged, positions which must not be contested, commands of the sovereign which must not be obeyed.

The non-dualistic mind says:

Practitioners of non-war know that the roads that must not be followed are those that lead one further into the jungle of dualistic illusions. They know that attacking any army or besieging any town only ties oneself further to the dualistic struggle. They know that contesting a position through force or deception only puts oneself on the treadmill of struggle and suffering. They know that the commands of a sovereign who is trapped in duality – and who does not have the non-dualistic moral law – must never be obeyed.

Practitioners of non-war are ever-vigilant toward the many subtle or overt temptations that seek to draw them into the dualistic struggle. They know that each step toward the struggle only separates oneself further from the abundant life that the Infinite is willing to bestow upon anyone who accepts it. Those who think they have to take something through force obviously cannot accept what is given freely.

The dualistic mind says:

So, the student of war who is unversed in the art of war of varying his plans, even though he be acquainted with the Five Advantages, will fail to make the best use of his men.

The non-dualistic mind says:

Practitioners of non-war understand the fundamental truth that the dualistic mind is forever trapped in the game of fighting a self-created enemy. Those blinded by duality will continue to project contradictory mental images into the cosmic mirror, and the mirror can only interpret this as a wish to experience an ongoing struggle.

When the mirror returns material circumstances that cause people to have to struggle against an external enemy, many use this as a confirmation that life on Earth truly *is* a struggle. They then focus all their energies on fighting the external enemy, while failing to see that it was their own mental images that precipitated the struggle.

This struggle against the external enemy causes people to form mental images which communicate to the cosmic mirror that they want to experience an even more intense struggle. The mirror can only give people what they say they want, and thus a downward spiral is created. People respond to the exterior struggle by creating mental images that precipitate an even more intense struggle, and this continues indefinitely.

Those who are blinded by duality will not take responsibility for themselves and admit that it is their own mental state which precipitates the struggle. They become so trapped in the art of war that they refuse not only to vary their battle plans, but they refuse to step back and recognize that for the struggle to end, they must change their state of consciousness.

Some even fall prey to a most dangerous illusion, namely that the only way to bring permanent peace is to fight the ultimate war that completely destroys the enemy. They then participate in the ultimate form of insanity, which is that one keeps doing the same thing while expecting that – some day – one will reap a different result. One continues to project the same mental image into the cosmic mirror, while thinking that one day the mirror will reflect back different material circumstances. One continues to project images of war, while thinking that, one day, peace will be the result.

This is comparable to a person sitting in front of a mirror and wanting the image in the mirror to smile while refusing to smile at the mirror.

Practitioners of non-war have seen through this common illusion. They know that if one is experiencing undesirable circumstances, one must change one's state of mind and send a different mental image into the cosmic mirror.

Practitioners of non-war are practical realists who understand that they might have sent dualistic images into the mirror for a long time. Therefore, changing one's state of mind will not have an immediate effect, for the new mental images must first cycle through the three higher levels of the material universe – the identity, mental and emotional level – before they can manifest as physical circumstances.

Practitioners of non-war will not simply turn the other cheek once and expect an immediate result. Nor will they give up if results are not forthcoming. They will keep turning the other cheek, and they will forgive seventy times seven. Thus, in their patience they will possess their souls. For the Infinite is – in the cycles of time and space – a rewarder of those that diligently seek it.

Practitioners of non-war also use appropriate techniques for invoking spiritual energy to consume the imperfect impulses they have sent out in the past. By consuming such impulses as they cycle through the higher layers of the material world, they can prevent them from manifesting as physical circumstances.

The dualistic mind says:

Hence in the wise leader's plans, considerations of advantage and of disadvantage will be blended together.
If our expectation of advantage be tempered in this way, we may succeed in accomplishing the essential part of our schemes.

The non-dualistic mind says:

The truly wise leader knows that although a finite advantage can be gained through the dualistic struggle, such an advantage can never be lasting. And since any participation in the struggle separates oneself from the abundant life of the Infinite, a finite advantage attained through dualistic means is truly a disadvantage. Things are never what they seem to the dualistic mind.

The truly wise leader knows that by opening oneself to the wisdom and energy of the Infinite, the abundant life can be attained. This requires one to give up the power and control one has attained in the finite world. To the unawakened mind, this will seem like a disadvantage. Yet it is truly the only road to achieving an incomparable and lasting advantage. Once again, things are not as they seem to the unawakened mind.

The dualistic mind says:

If, on the other hand, in the midst of difficulties we are always ready to seize an advantage, we may extricate ourselves from misfortune.

The non-dualistic mind says:

Practitioners of non-war are not above experiencing difficulties, for they live in a world where most people still exercise their free will through the filter of the dualistic mind. Yet they know that seeking a finite advantage over others is not the way to extricate oneself from misfortune. The only way to truly rise above misfortune is to seek union with the Infinite.

The dualistic mind says:

The art of war teaches us to rely not on the likelihood of the enemy not coming, but on our own readiness to receive him; not on the chance of his not attacking, but rather on the fact that we have made our position unassailable.

The non-dualistic mind says:

Practitioners of non-war have accepted full responsibility for themselves and are therefore focused on expanding their own consciousness rather than seeking to change others.

When they experience opposition from others, they first look for a cause within themselves and seek to resolve any internal resistance that will precipitate external resistance. Yet they also realize that even those who have removed the beam from their own eyes will encounter resistance from others.

As long as there are people who are blinded by duality, they will resist even those who are awakened. This is allowed so that those who are awakened may have an opportunity to awaken others. Practitioners of non-war know that their only chance of awakening others is to never respond in a dualistic manner.

Practitioners of non-war never respond to resistance with more resistance. Instead, they surrender all finite resistance and make their position truly unassailable through oneness with the Infinite.

The dualistic mind says:

There are five dangerous faults which may affect a general: (1) Recklessness, which leads to destruction; (2) Cowardice, which leads to capture; (3) A hasty temper, which can be provoked by insults; (4) A delicacy of honor which is sensitive to shame; (5) Over-solicitude for his men, which exposes him to worry and trouble.

These are the five besetting sins of a general, ruinous to the conduct of war.

When an army is overthrown and its leader slain, the cause will surely be found among these five dangerous faults. Let them be a subject of meditation.

The non-dualistic mind says:

Practitioners of non-war recognize that there are more than five dangerous faults, for the temptations of the dualistic mind are as innumerable as they are subtle. Thus, they do not meditate on how to avoid specific faults in a finite war but on how to rise above the entire consciousness of duality by seeking oneness with the Infinite.

Chapter 9.
The Warriors of Peace on the March

The dualistic mind says:

We come now to the question of encamping the army, and observing signs of the enemy.

The non-dualistic mind says

Practitioners of non-war, having been awakened from the illusions of duality, have risen above the temptations to fight a finite battle against a finite enemy. They also recognize that beyond the physical wars being fought on Earth, there is a non-physical "war" for the minds and hearts of the people.

This war is being "fought" between two forces, although only one of those forces is fighting in a dualistic manner. The two forces are:

- **The Force of Oneness.** These are beings who are united with the Infinite and are existing in the realm that is above the four levels of the material universe. Some call it Heaven, some call it the spiritual realm.

    Some of these beings once descended to Earth to serve as examples. They came to demonstrate that all people – being created in the image and likeness of the Infinite – have the potential to attain direct, inner union with the Infinite and thus either ascend to the spiritual realm or serve as open doors for raising the material universe to the abundance of the Infinite. These beings serve as the teachers of humankind and are using non-dualistic means to awaken people from the illusions of duality and help them rise above the finite struggle.

These ascended beings have infinite creative powers, yet because they are not in a physical body, they do not have authority to use those powers on Earth. Thus, they must work through those in embodiment who choose to align themselves with the Force of Oneness and become open doors for the wisdom and energy of the Infinite. The spiritual teachers have the power – but not the authority – to change the Earth. People in embodiment have the authority—but not the power. Thus, only when a critical mass of people come into oneness with their spiritual teachers, will the Earth be changed—as in the twinkling of an eye. Only then shall the last trumpet of war have sounded.

- **The Forces of Separation.** These are beings who have refused to come into oneness with the Infinite. They are not able to ascend to the spiritual realm, in which there is no division. Many of them have lost their opportunity to embody on Earth and thus reside in the non-physical levels of the material universe, from which they seek to influence the thoughts and feelings of human beings.

Many of these beings have in the past been in embodiment on Earth and served as examples of how far people are willing to go in selfish pursuits. They have been directly responsible for most of the wars and atrocities seen in history. They are allowed to remain with the Earth because so many people are still blinded by the dualistic illusions and have thus made themselves the blind followers of the blind leaders. As long as there are students of the art of war, there will be teachers of the art of war.

Those who make up the Forces of Separation likewise have no direct authority to act on Earth. They can work only through people who have become blinded by duality and thus – knowingly or unknowingly – have made themselves instruments for the dualistic mind.

Why do those who belong to the Forces of Separation seek control over the people on Earth? Because in cutting themselves off from the Infinite, they are no longer able to receive the life-sustaining energy directly from the Infinite. To stay alive, they must steal this energy from those who still receive it from the source. They do this by fooling people into believing in dualistic illusions, whereby they qualify the pure energy of the Infinite with an imperfect vibration, such as fear, anger or other limiting emotions. The pure light cannot be absorbed by those who belong to the Forces of Separation—only the impure light that has been lowered in vibration.

The Forces of Separation are also driven by an anger against the Infinite and a desire to prove that they can exist – forever – in a world of their own making, a world that is separated from the Infinite. It is their goal to turn planet Earth into such a world, and presently they have managed to make most people accept the illusions of duality. Thus, the Earth has descended far below its original state of purity and abundance. The reason being that people continue to project into the cosmic mirror images that are based on the illusion of separation.

These forces may also be called the force of peace and the forces of war. The force of peace is one force of united beings. The forces of war are many, for they are divided amongst themselves, even within themselves. There is a constant warring in their members.

Practitioners of non-war see the essential battle for the minds of the people. Having chosen to align themselves with the force of peace, they know they are on Earth to serve as the open doors for the incomparable, non-dualistic wisdom that will set the people free from the illusions of duality.

Practitioners of non-war know that in this pursuit, they must be wise as serpents, harmless as doves. They must be able to see through the dualistic illusions, so they can expose the forces of war and set the people free from their lies. Yet in doing so, they must *never* respond in a dualistic manner, for this will only give energy to the forces of war.

Practitioners of non-war must do right action while remaining non-attached to the fruits of action—this is being harmless as a dove. Practitioners of non-war are not here to override the free choices of the people, for that is the method of the forces of war.

Practitioners of non-war are here to give people a free choice by showing them that there is something beyond the dualistic illusions. Currently, most people have never encountered anything beyond duality, and thus they have never had the opportunity to choose between a dualistic "truth" and the non-dualistic wisdom of the Infinite.

Practitioners of non-war are here to give people that choice without choosing *for* them. If people – after having been given a real choice – prefer to continue following the forces of war, then even that choice must be respected. For only when you remain non-attached, will the prince of war come and have nothing in you.

Practitioners of non-war know that the River of Life moves on. Human beings on Earth cannot stop the river forever, but they can slow it down for a time. Thus, it is inevitable that the forces of war will lose their grip on planet Earth. The people can chose to give their power to the forces of war and thus keep them alive for a time. They have done so for thousands of years, and if they prefer to continue to do so, their choice must be accepted.

In the finite world, everything that is separated from the Infinite must come to an end. The Golden Age of peace will eventually come. The question of when is decided by how many people are willing to awaken themselves from the illusions of duality and become practitioners of the art of non-war.

***

Practitioners of non-war know that the present time presents a unique opportunity for exposing the forces of war for all to see. This is due to several factors:

- In recorded history there has not been a time when people have had a greater understanding of the world than today. Thus, they have a better foundation for understanding how the forces of war and the illusions of duality have influenced every area of society.

- Modern people have a greater understanding of psychology, which gives them a better foundation for understanding how the illusions of duality have influenced their own minds. Many modern people are well-equipped for discovering and removing the beam in their own eye.

- The weapons of war are more destructive than ever, which gives people a greater incentive for preventing war. Nuclear power has taught people that in some cases the destruction that would result from a war will outweigh any potential advantages.

- Humanity has been prepared by the force of peace to be awakened, thereby realizing that true and lasting peace cannot be attained through finite means. It can be attained *only* by people seeing through the illusions of duality and learning how to draw upon the power, wisdom and love of the Infinite.

- Humanity has a greater understanding of energy and the fact that matter is made from energy. This means that modern people are prepared to understand that there is no barrier between mind and matter, which means that the minds of human beings can influence the physical planet. Human actions can create pollution, but human thoughts and feelings have an even more profound effect on the physical planet.

Many people are ready to understand that this explains the increased frequency and intensity of some natural disasters. Many are ready to understand that it is time for modern people to learn how to work *with* the Earth instead of seeking to subdue it through force. Practitioners of war see nature and the physical planet as an enemy that must be conquered. Practitioners of non-war see the Earth as their ally and learn how to work *with* it instead of *against* it.

Practitioners of non-war see the unique opportunity for being part of a large-scale awakening. They also see that this does not mean that all people will suddenly accept the same belief system, religion or political philosophy. Treating people like sheep and seeking to force them all into the same fold is a dualistic illusion.

Practitioners of non-war see beyond all outer thought systems and philosophies. They see that what is needed at this time is for people to be awakened to the universal truth of the Infinite. This is a Living Truth that can never be confined to any belief system on Earth. The Infinite can never be forced into a mental box on Earth, so only those who are willing to reach beyond all mental boxes can experience the Infinite.

Practitioners of non-war know that the Infinite is a Spirit and must be experienced in Spirit and in truth. They are not working to force a particular belief system upon people. They are working to help people see the universal truth beyond all finite belief systems.

This does not mean that practitioners of non-war are fighting against finite belief systems. They recognize that many belief systems contain elements of truth. Practitioners of non-war are seeking to help others see the Infinite truth beyond their belief system, which helps people see that the Infinite truth can have many finite expressions.

Only when people see this basic truth, can they join the River of Life that is constantly transcending itself and becoming MORE. Only in perpetual self-transcendence can one find the abundant life.

***

Practitioners of non-war never see other people as enemies. They realize that they are not fighting other people or even belief systems and institutions. Their real goal is to expose the finite forces that seek to enslave people and the Infinite forces that seek to set them free.

Yet practitioners of non-war also realize that many people have become so blinded by the illusions of duality that they think such illusions represent the truth. Thus, they will resist any attempt to bring forth non-dualistic wisdom, even labeling it as the works of the devil or as religious superstition.

Many people will resist the exposure of the true causes of war, for they are not willing to cast out the beam from their own eye. Many people have come to believe that they gain some advantage from war or that war is a justifiable means for pursuing a particular end.

Practitioners of non-war see that there are certain groups of people who have become so blinded by duality that they have become practitioners of the art of war. These are the main groupings of the practitioners of war:

- The sovereign represents the leaders who see war as a means to a political end. They may claim to be fighting for a worthy cause, but in most cases it is a smokescreen for their real cause, which is to secure or maintain their own privilege and power. They would never participate in war but let others fight for them. They often have little if any regard for the cost in human lives and suffering. Many sovereigns do not want to let go of war as a tool for expanding or securing their power.

- The merchants of war are those who see war mainly as a means to obtain profit. They will supply arms to anyone who can pay, regardless of causes or consequences. They will gladly supply arms to both sides of a conflict if possible. They will even create a conflict in order to sell arms, and they are skilled at manipulating both the political leaders and the people in creating such a conflict. They have absolutely no regard for the cost of human lives and suffering. The merchants of war obviously do not want war to disappear from planet Earth.

- The generals represent those for whom the art of war has become a calling beyond just making a living. These are the professional soldiers who take pride in excelling at the art of war. They will fight any war that their sovereign commands them to fight, believing they have no need to evaluate the moral implications. They have a marginal regard for the cost of war, for they are prepared to sacrifice almost any amount of soldiers necessary to defeat the enemy. Their primary objective is to obtain a finite victory over a finite enemy. In fact, they are the ones most trapped in the belief that there is an enemy, for without an enemy there would be no justification for their existence or their craft. These warriors likewise do not want to see war disappear.

- The soldiers are those who always do most of the fighting and dying. Some soldiers are forced into service and thus quite aware of the human cost of war. Some are looking at military service as a way to make a living or as a way of life. Some are motivated by patriotism and think being loyal to a finite country is more important than being loyal to the Infinite. Some believe they are fighting for a just cause and think being loyal to a worthy cause is more important than being loyal to the Infinite, who decreed, "Thou shalt not kill!" Many soldiers feel trapped and would be happy to see war disappear.

- The people are the ones who bear the economical and much of the human cost of war. They might be killed by war, have their lives destroyed or – at the very least – lose loved ones. They always pay the financial cost of war. Many among the people have come to believe the lie that war is inevitable and that there is no other way to respond to certain situations than through war. Others are like the soldiers and are loyal to their country, its sovereign or to a cause they believe justifies the means of war. As with many soldiers, most people have regard for the value of human life and are well aware of the human cost of war. While some among the people will hold on to the belief that war is necessary, many can be awakened to the non-dualistic truth about war. Once awakened, they will gladly see war disappear from this planet.

Practitioners of non-war know that the probability of awakening the different groups among the practitioners of war is as follows:

- The sovereign. It can be very difficult to awaken the political leaders to the folly of war. Such people are very reluctant to admit that they have made a mistake. Some are so convinced of their right to power and privilege that they will never listen to anyone they consider below them in rank—and some leaders consider anybody to be below them. A few leaders can be awakened by coming to understand how they have been blinded by the illusions of duality or manipulated by the merchants of war. Some can be awakened through a genuine regard for the lives and suffering of the people.

- The merchants are the most difficult to awaken. They are so firmly blinded by the never-ending craving for profit that they are unreachable with higher reason. Only the experience of having their lives ruined by their own greed can occasionally awaken a merchant of war.

- The professional soldiers are likewise difficult to awaken, for it would require them to admit that they have been living a lie and that their entire lives have been built on an unjust and illusory foundation. Yet they can sometimes be awakened by seeing the folly of a dualistic sovereign or the greed of the merchants. Some can be awakened through a genuine regard for their soldiers or the people they kill during war.

- The soldiers are far more likely to be awakened as they know the cost of war, often on their own bodies and minds. Yet they must be helped to see that loyalty to any cause or institution in the finite world must be second to loyalty to the incomparable moral law of the Infinite. Soldiers are often awakened when they experience that they were not treated as individuals but were seen as expendable by their superiors or their political leaders—or were let down by society after the war. They can also be awakened by helping them see that they were not truly fighting for a just cause but were simply pawns in the geopolitical game played by the ruling elite and the merchants of death.

- The people are the most likely to be awakened to the folly of war. The people are the key to a planetary change, for without their support, the political leaders, the merchants and the generals could not continue to wage war. No leaders have more power than what the people give them. Leaders are a reflection of the consciousness of the people, and thus the key to a change in leadership is to change the collective consciousness away from the belief that war is necessary, unavoidable or beneficial. There are many ways to reach the people, and the practitioners of non-war seek to work with people individually.

Practitioners of non-war focus their attention and energy according to this assessment, starting with the people and the soldiers.

***

The most important insight to give people is that war is not inevitable. It is an artificial creation of the forces of war. These forces have no real power over the people. They can exist only as long as the people give them power. To fool people into giving them power, the forces of war must keep people in ignorance.

As soon as the people start seeing through the illusions of the dualistic mind, they can stop giving their power to the forces of war. Thereby, the power of these forces will gradually be depleted, and they will lose their iron grip on the collective consciousness.

Up until this point in history, the forces of war have managed to remain hidden, and that is why they have continued to pull the people into believing that certain wars were necessary, just or unavoidable. Humanity is now on the verge of an awakening that will create an upward spiral and momentum. This can – very quickly – lead to the forces of war losing their power to create further wars, thus ushering in a Golden Age of peace, an age of both material and spiritual abundance.

Practitioners of non-war hold the vision of such a Golden Age. Because they are attuned to the Infinite, they know it is a real possibility in the short term and an inevitable certainty in the long term. They work toward making it a certainty in their own lifetimes, for they know the acceptable time is NOW.

Practitioners of war – warriors of war – seek honor in the finite world—the honor that comes from defeating one's enemy in a finite battle.

Practitioners of non-war – warriors of peace – seek the incomparable honor of the Infinite. This honor comes from helping other people attain oneness with the Infinite, thus replacing the finite struggle with the abundant life.

Which honor is more desirable to you?

Chapter 10.
Knowing Physical and Non-physical Terrain

The dualistic mind says:

We may distinguish six kinds of terrain, to wit: (1) Accessible ground; (2) entangling ground; (3) temporizing ground; (4) narrow passes; (5) precipitous heights; (6) positions at a great distance from the enemy.

The non-dualistic mind says:

Practitioners of non-war must also know the conditions currently found on Earth. This includes material conditions, but also the "terrain" of the mind, which means both the individual mind and the collective mind.

Practitioners of non-war see the reality that most people on Earth are blinded by the dualistic illusions. Thus, it is clear to them that the primary stratagem of the forces of war is to keep people trapped in ignorance.

In past ages, keeping people in ignorance meant that they knew nothing or very little. The modern information age proves that this strategy has failed. The forces of war have now reluctantly admitted that they cannot keep people in a state of knowing nothing. Instead, their new strategy is to misdirect people's quest for knowledge.

Ignorance does not mean that you know nothing. Ignorance means that you do not know who you are—you do not see yourself as an individual expression of the Infinite. Thus, you do not know or accept that you have the potential to become an open door for the power, wisdom and love of the Infinite. And this is precisely the form of ignorance that the forces of war want to maintain.

When you are ignorant of who you are, you cannot fulfill your intended role of having dominion over the Earth. By default, this gives dominion to the forces of war.

When you are in ignorance of your true identity, you cannot serve in bringing the kingdom of the Infinite into physical manifestation. Manifesting this kingdom is the *only* way to remove war and bring true peace.

This explains why the forces of war do not want people to fill the role of being the peacemakers. They want to maintain control of the Earth and keep it as a separate sphere, in which their self-defined, dualistic laws can supersede the moral law of the Infinite. They want duality to continue to reign on Earth, and they will resist any attempt to bring the non-dualistic, indivisible kingdom of the Infinite.

Practitioners of non-war understand that the members of the forces of war believe they own this planet. They are seeking to maintain it as a world in which the one moral law of the Infinite has been shut out. Thus, practitioners of war can define their own laws based on their self-interest. They can become a law unto themselves and make the people subject unto them.

Practitioners of non-war understand that those who are part of the forces of war will do anything in their power to prevent the people from awakening from the dualistic illusions that form the very foundation upon which the practitioners of war have built their finite empires. This includes using all institutions of society to perpetuate dualistic illusions.

***

Practitioners of non-war understand the fact that the practitioners of war and the immaterial forces of war have distorted all institutions of society in order to perpetuate the dualistic illusions. The purpose is to keep the people trapped in the basic dualistic illusion, namely that they are separated from the Infinite and that they live in a world that is separated from the Infinite. In order to become instruments for setting the people free from these illusions, practitioners of non-war study every aspect of how society has been influenced by the dualistic illusions.

Religious institutions

Practitioners of non-war have been awakened from the common illusion that religious institutions are somehow sacred and thus above being influenced by dualistic self-interest. They realize that religious institutions exist in the finite world and that anything in the finite world can be influenced by the dualistic mind.

Practitioners of non-war realize the truth that if anything *can* be influenced by the dualistic mind, it *will* be. The only defense is constant vigilance, whereby one connects to the wisdom of the Infinite, using it to expose the dualistic illusions. This is the primary role of practitioners of non-war.

Practitioners of non-war understand that for the forces of war, nothing is sacred. For them, everything is simply a means to an end.

The primary objective of the forces of war is to keep people trapped in the illusion that they are separated from the Infinite. And what better means for securing this end than using the very institutions that claim to be the connecting link between the people and their God?

Practitioners of non-war know that most religions were started by a prophet or visionary who had attained either a strong connection to the Infinite or oneness with the Infinite. Through that union, the person became the open door for bringing forth a new teaching that came directly from the Infinite.

Even a teaching that comes from the Infinite must be adapted to the consciousness of the people who are receiving it. For if the teaching is too far above the level of consciousness of the recipients, how can they grasp and accept it?

Even a teaching that comes from the Infinite must be clothed in the words used in the finite world, and this makes it subject to finite interpretations. Different people will interpret the teaching based on their state of consciousness, often coloring it with the dualistic illusions they have come to accept.

Practitioners of non-war, therefore, see the fact that even a teaching coming from the Infinite is not meant to be absolute, infallible or never-changing. For how could anything be absolute in the finite world?

A spiritual teaching is not meant to be an end in itself – for that makes it a graven image – but a means to an end, namely a direct experience of the Infinite. The true purpose of a spiritual teaching is that people use it as a ladder for climbing closer to a direct encounter with the Infinite. Only by transcending the outer teaching, will people enter the kingdom of the Infinite that is within them.

A spiritual teaching is meant to help people discover and expand their direct inner connection to the Infinite. Yet any teaching can be perverted by the illusions of duality. This happens when people do not use the teaching as a tool for having a direct encounter with the wisdom of the Infinite. Instead, they turn the outer teaching into a closed system that is the only source of knowledge.

The dualistic illusions will cause some people to elevate a finite teaching to the status of infallibility, thus believing that as long as they follow the outer teaching, their salvation is guaranteed. This dream of an automatic salvation will be believed by those who will not take responsibility for themselves. Thus, they will not admit that outer actions cannot get you into the inner kingdom. Only an inner transformation of consciousness will get you into the kingdom, for the kingdom of the Infinite is within you.

Some people will interpret the words of a teaching based on their present state of consciousness instead of using the words as a springboard for transcending that state of consciousness. They will reason that their teaching and their interpretation is superior to any other teaching or interpretation, and they have now turned the spiritual teaching into a graven image. It will not be long before the dualistic mind tempts them into using it as a weapon against other people.

A graven image can be used to attain a sense of superiority over others or to justify aggression against others.

Thus, even a spiritual teaching can be used as a justification for war, often as a smokescreen for disguising the ongoing dualistic struggle. What better way to motivate people for going to war than making them believe they are fighting for God's cause? Ultimate motivation leads to ultimate sacrifice—and ultimate blindness.

Some people will elevate the person who brought forth the spiritual teaching to the status of being God incarnate or being the only one who could ever reach a certain state of perfection. Practitioners of non-war know that any visionary came to set forth an example that all people can follow. True spiritual leaders have come to show that all people have the potential to attain union with the Infinite—out of which they sprang.

Practitioners of non-war see that by elevating a spiritual leader to the status of an idol, his or her example is instantly destroyed. The leader is now an exception rather than an example, an idol to worship rather than a leader to follow and emulate. Practitioners of non-war also see that this idolatry is a violation of the commandments to never put any finite expression before the Infinite and to always look beyond any finite images, lest they become graven – unchanging – images.

Practitioners of non-war see that this is a complete subversion of the purpose for which the spiritual leader was sent to Earth. The leader came to help all people escape the prison of duality by showing them how to follow a systematic path that leads to the kingdom of the Infinite. Practitioners of non-war seek to help others escape the idol worship that blocks their entry into the inner kingdom.

Practitioners of non-war seek to free others from the perversions of religion without causing them to jump into the opposite dualistic extreme of rejecting all religion and spirituality. They seek to help people see that practitioners of war have often managed to pervert religious institutions. This is done by changing the original teaching so it now seems people do not have direct access to the Infinite within themselves but need an external institution in order to be saved.

The forces of war are always seeking ultimate authority over the people. And what better way to attain it than through a religious institution that claims it has the power to send people to Heaven—or to hell. Few religious institutions are untouched by this, yet the original teaching – in its pure form – is still a valid way to move closer to a direct experience of the Infinite.

Practitioners of non-war also seek to help others see that all true religions came from the same source, namely the force of peace that is made up of beings who are united with the Infinite. Thus, there can be more than one true religion, for all true religions seeks to help their followers reach beyond finite expressions and attain union with the Infinite.

When the members of each religion follow their prescribed way toward union with the Infinite, they will grow ever closer to union with each other. Thus, there will be no basis for conflict or war between different religions. Only dualistic religions can create conflict. No dualistic religion can be a true religion, for duality can never come from the Infinite.

Practitioners of non-war may be members of a finite religion and honor its scriptures and tradition. Yet their primary religion is the incomparable religion of the Infinite. People who flow with this River of Life are always united—regardless of finite appearances.

Scientific institutions

Practitioners of non-war see that human beings have an inherent longing for something better, a sense that there must be more to life than what they are experiencing right now. This longing comes from the fact that people are extensions of the Infinite and thus have a built-in longing to return to their source. This longing can be diverted or suppressed, but it can never be completely extinguished.

One expression of this longing is the quest for knowledge, the drive to understand oneself and the world. There are two primary expressions of this quest for knowledge, namely spirituality and science.

Spirituality is – in its pure form – a quest to understand the Infinite and oneself as an expression of the Infinite. This understanding forms the foundation for becoming an open door, whereby the wisdom and energy of the Infinite can flow into this world and transform the current limitations into the abundant life.

Yet for the flow of wisdom and energy to have the maximum effect in transforming this world, it must be expressed through a thorough understanding of the material world. Science is – in its pure form – a quest to learn how to combine knowledge of the Infinite with knowledge of the finite. The purpose is to direct the energy of the Infinite into producing the highest possible state of both spiritual and material abundance on Earth.

Practitioners of non-war understand the two basic forces that make up the world of form, namely the expanding and the contracting force, the father and mother aspect of the Infinite. Spirituality is father, science is mother. Only when the two come together in harmony, can a new life be born.

Based on this understanding of the highest role of spirituality and science, practitioners of non-war clearly see how science has been perverted into perpetuating the lie of separation. If the Infinite does not exist and if humans are merely highly evolved animals, then how could people have the potential to reconnect with their infinite source?

A science that is separated from the wisdom of the Infinite, will inevitably create moral and ethical problems that seem to have no solution. For without the nondualistic guiding rod of the Infinite, what is to prevent science from becoming a pawn in the human power play? Surely, the merchants of war will want science to create ever more powerful weapons, as well as technology that results in environmental problems.

If all humans are merely evolved animals, what is to prevent the most "fit" humans from using science to attain greater power and control? This explains why science has been the instrument for increasing the destructive power of the weapons of war to a point that would have shocked Sun Tzu to the marrow of his bones. Who is to tell science that what *can* be done is not always what *should* be done—who but the Infinite that is above all human self-interest?

Practitioners of non-war seek to free others from the perversions of science without causing them to jump into the opposite dualistic extreme of rejecting all need for science. They do this by helping people see that even science has been perverted by the dualistic mind. For only this mind could cause scientists to deny the existence of something beyond the material universe.

Political institutions

Practitioners of non-war know that, to the forces of war, anything is a means to an end. All can see how totalitarian governments have been used to suppress and enslave the people, for history is littered with examples of this. Yet practitioners of non-war see that even democratic governments can be used to perpetuate the illusion of separation.

One example is the belief in the separation of church and state. The reality behind this concept is that no one religion must be allowed to control a democratic government. Yet this does not mean that a democratic government must be separated from the wisdom and the moral law of the Infinite, the Infinite that is beyond any religion on Earth. For if there is no respect for a superior source of human rights, how can one prevent a government from thinking it can define or violate the rights of the people?

Democracy is based on the concept of inalienable rights. Yet if people's rights are defined by any finite institution – be it a church or a state – then those rights will soon be subverted. They will be overruled by those who are so blinded by the dualistic mind that they think they are a law unto themselves and can thus define the rights of the people.

Inalienable rights can come from only one source, namely the Infinite. They can be secured *only* by a gov-

160

ernment that recognizes the Infinite and is aligned with the non-dualistic moral law of the Infinite.

Freedom without the Infinite must of necessity be a finite freedom. And a freedom that is based on finite conditions can be taken away by finite forces. Freedom based on unity with the Infinite is incomparable freedom.

Another dualistic illusion perpetuated by democratic institutions is the idea that the people cannot govern themselves but need a ruling elite. This is the same illusion that has been used to justify all totalitarian rulers, only it has been given a democratic disguise.

The lie behind this illusion is that the people are somehow deficient and thus do not have what it takes to govern their nation. Only the members of a small elite have what it takes, and thus the elite should be allowed to rule.

This philosophy can be based on both a religious or a scientific underpinning. If people are believed to be mortal sinners, then obviously they cannot rule themselves but need church leaders. If people are believed to be only evolved animals, then obviously those who are most "fit" should be allowed to rule.

Practitioners of non-war see the reality that all people are individualizations of the Infinite, and thus all have the potential to become open doors for the power, wisdom and love of the Infinite. When people are taught how to connect themselves to the Infinite, they are perfectly capable of governing themselves—for it will be the Infinite governing through them.

Practitioners of non-war work to expose elitism in all of its subtle disguises and seek to help the people connect to the Infinite within themselves. They seek to help people see that many political ideologies have been so influenced by the dualistic illusions that they have been used by the power elite to maintain or expand their power while they remain hidden to the people. This explains why so many people see that something is wrong with society but fail to understand why certain problems continue to exist. These problems have not been solved because the elite do not want them to be solved.

Practitioners of non-war seek to free others from the perversions of politics without causing them to jump into the opposite dualistic extreme of rejecting all politics as corrupt. For if the good people withdraw from politics, the self-centered members of the elite will inevitably rule. And they are the ones who have perverted politics by causing it to be influenced by – even based on – dualistic self-interest instead of enlightened self-interest.

Members of the power elite see politics as a means to an end, which is often the end of raising themselves up in comparison to the people by keeping the people down. Practitioners of non-war see politics as a way to raise up everyone and give the abundant life to all people.

Educational institutions

Practitioners of non-war understand that education has often been used by the ruling elite to perpetuate the dualistic illusions that keep the elite in power. Education is a powerful means for maintaining status quo by making the people believe in certain illusions that make change seem impossible or undesirable.

Education might promote the religious belief that people are separated from God or the scientific belief that people are evolved animals. Yet beyond such illusions, most educational institutions are based on the even more subtle illusion that knowledge can be obtained only through finite institutions, such as a church or science.

Most education is based on the concept that people cannot obtain true knowledge on their own but must be told by experts what is true and false, valid and invalid.

Practitioners of non-war know that all people have access to the wisdom of the Infinite – the key of knowledge – within themselves. Thus, they seek to counteract the dualistic illusions of the lawyers that are designed to take the key of knowledge away from the people.

The media

Practitioners of non-war know that the forces of war have always formed an elite who think they are above the people. The elite can control the people only through ignorance. In previous ages, this meant withholding information and suppressing all information that challenged the ruling elite and their philosophy.

In today's age, this is no longer possible, and it is not even necessary. Members of the elite do not have to keep the people in a state of knowing nothing—they only have to keep them in a state of being ignorant of their true identity and potential.

Practitioners of non-war understand that members of the ruling elite always seek to control the media. They use it to perpetuate the dualistic illusions that keep the elite in power and prevent their philosophy from being challenged or questioned. The media is also used to perpetuate a world view that is based on dualistic illusions and thus keeps the people from challenging the dualistic mind and the power elite.

Practitioners of non-war seek to set the people free from the dualistic lies being perpetuated through mainstream media. In doing so, they expect no help from mainstream media, instead seeking non-mainstream ways of perpetuating information.

Practitioners of non-war understand that mainstream media is also perpetuating the lie that the people cannot know truth within themselves, thus needing to rely on experts to define knowledge and the media to distribute it.

Practitioners of non-war are not seeking to usurp the position of the media and set themselves up as experts. They are seeking to awaken people to the fact that they have the key of knowledge and can access the wisdom of the Infinite within themselves.

This does not mean that experts are not needed, but it does mean that true experts are those who recognize the reality of the Infinite instead of denying its existence. One becomes a real expert only by removing the beam of duality and separation from one's own eye.

Military institutions

Military institutions are based on and thus perpetuate at least some of the following dualistic illusions:

- War is an unavoidable reality; it is simply part of life on planet Earth.

- No nation can exist or survive without a military.

- War is the only way to solve certain conflicts.

- War is a necessary, justified or beneficial way to respond to certain situations. In some situations there simply is no other response than war.

- War can be a justifiable means for achieving a greater good. It is possible, even necessary, to do evil that good may come.

- Sustainable gain and permanent survival can be achieved through war.

- War is a way for both individuals and nations to pursue glory and honor.

- Killing other people can give soldiers valor and honor.

- Killing other people can lead to benefits in Heaven, be it 70 virgins or an eternity with Christ.

- War can lead to permanent peace by destroying those who work against peace. If only all enemies are killed, then peace will be the automatic result.

Practitioners of non-war see the fallacy of these illusions, and they are working to help other people see this as well.

Practitioners of non-war see through the primary illusion that in some situations war is the only response. They know that when people think they have no other response than war, it is because they have become blinded by the dualistic mind, which has created a "fog of war."

Such a state of spiritual blindness can exist *only* because people do not know that they have direct access to the wisdom of the Infinite. For when this wisdom is brought into a situation, people will see that they are *never* in a situation where the only possible response is war.

With the wisdom of the Infinite, it is possible to resolve *any* situation without war. For surely, the Infinite has the wisdom to make it possible for people to follow its own command, "Thou shalt not kill!"

In any situation, the obvious alternative to war is to turn the other cheek, thereby facilitating the judgment of the aggressor. Doing this is aligning oneself with the greater purpose of the Infinite. Resorting to war is separating oneself from the Infinite. The latter can never lead to permanent gain, whereas the former leads to incomparable gain.

Practitioners of non-war see through the illusion that it is possible to create a permanent state of peace through war. The dualistic "logic" is that if only all enemies are killed, peace will automatically follow.

Practitioners of non-war understand the nature of duality. They know that *any* use of military force will send an impulse into the cosmic mirror that will inevitably generate an opposing force. The very act of seeking to destroy one enemy will inevitably create the next enemy.

Any nation which resorts to military force is essentially sending a signal into the cosmic mirror that it wants to experience a state of perpetual war or the threat of war. And the cosmic mirror is bound by the law of free will to comply with the wishes of any nation.

Destroying a physical tyrant through war will not remove the real tyrant. In fact, it will only strengthen the real tyrant. That tyrant is the forces of war – many of which are non-physical – and the dualistic mind, which is entirely non-physical. Any violent act generates negative energy that only feeds the beast of war.

Practitioners of non-war understand this basic reality, and they seek to awaken other people to the fact that the only way to avoid war, the only way to attain true and lasting peace, is for a nation to send a non-violent impulse into the cosmic mirror. This can be attained only by those who refuse to respond to *any* situation through military force. Instead, they turn the other cheek and let the law of God exact its inevitable vengeance.

"Vengeance is mine," saith the Infinite "my law of action and reaction will repay." Practitioners of non-war trust the law of the Infinite and know they have no need to punish or exact vengeance regardless of the actions of other people. In fact, by doing so, one only binds oneself to the dualistic struggle. Only those who believe in the illusion of separation do not trust the law of the Infinite.

Practitioners of non-war understand that humanity has reached a crucial turning point, where there is an unprecedented opportunity for exposing and dismissing the forces of war and the dualistic illusions behind them.

They even understand that the time has come for some nations to take the consequence and disband their military forces. This will serve to set a global example that these nations are willing to raise themselves above the planetary madness that sees war as a solution. There is no more powerful way for a nation to align itself with the Infinite.

Business institutions

Practitioners of non-war see that even business institutions and philosophies have been used to perpetuate dualistic illusions. One such illusion is the lie that people on Earth can create wealth only through finite means.

Practitioners of non-war see that this illusion is promoted because only wealth created through finite means can be controlled by a finite elite. They also see that there is a power elite whose members want ultimate control of Earth, and they would rather keep the majority of the world's population in poverty than open the floodgates to the uncontrollable abundance of the Infinite.

Practitioners of non-war see that there is a power elite whose members have an insatiable desire to feel better than others. This elite does not want the abundant life manifest on Earth. They want a state of lack, which gives rise to inequality. For the elite to be rich, the people have to be poor.

Practitioners of non-war see that permanent peace cannot be achieved as long as a majority of the world's population is kept in poverty. Yet the only way to remove poverty is to change the status quo in which the majority of the world's resources and wealth is concentrated under the control of a small elite.

Any financial institution and philosophy that is serving – directly or indirectly – to uphold the unequal distribution of wealth – concentrating it in the control of a small elite, even a small elite of nations – is working directly against peace.

Practitioners of non-war also see that the higher way to change the unequal distribution of wealth is *not* a political solution that concentrates wealth in the control of the state. For this will only concentrate wealth in the hands of those who control the state.

The true way to overcome elitism in the economy is to awaken all people to their potential to bring forth wisdom and energy directly from the Infinite within themselves. This will increase the amount of wealth beyond what can be controlled by any elite, and thus it will lead to true economic freedom and abundance for all.

**

Practitioners of non-war see that one of the most crippling lies about business is that it is based upon and driven by competition. This lie springs directly from the consciousness of lack, the belief that the Earth has only a finite amount of resources.

Once blinded by the illusion of lack, a business becomes obsessed with the competition from other businesses. This ties up most of its resources in staying ahead of or even destroying the competition.

The business now becomes swallowed up in the dualistic struggle that will inevitably lead to its demise. This explains why even the largest of businesses will eventually stagnate and collapse, either through external competition or internal disintegration.

When a business becomes obsessed with competing against other businesses, it becomes a closed system. It shuts itself off from the wisdom and energy of the Infinite and thus loses its creativity. This makes the business subject to the opposing dualistic forces that will inevitably break it down.

It is a cosmic law that anything which becomes a closed system – anything that loses creativity and the will to reinvent itself – will inevitably disintegrate. A business may resist this law for a time, but only for a time.

The truly successful businesses are those who are based on the wisdom of the Infinite. Thus, instead of competing with other businesses for a greater slice of the finite pie, they devote all of their resources to innovation—the bringing forth of wisdom and energy directly from the Infinite. This expands the pie beyond all boundaries, for such businesses see that all boundaries are boundaries of imagination.

In the present age the most successful businesses will be those who raise themselves above the illusion of competition and unite their efforts in a creative pursuit of new sources of abundance for all. These businesses will come together in a non-dualistic spirit of cooperation, for they see that they can precipitate more abundance when united than when divided.

There is no greater lie in business than the dream of a monopoly, for this can be attained only by creating an artificial scarcity. Such a scarcity can be created only by cutting off a society, perhaps an entire planet, from the wisdom and energy of the Infinite.

Even if this could be achieved, it would turn the planet into a closed system. By the time a business had finally attained the ultimate monopoly – the dream of some capitalists – the entire system would collapse from within.

Practitioners of non-war in business see clearly that those who are trapped in the illusions of duality are working very hard to kill the goose that lays the golden eggs. Practitioners of non-war give up such finite pursuits and focus on learning how to precipitate golden eggs directly from the Infinite.

History

Practitioners of non-war understand the fact that history is written by the winners. Thus, history is written to perpetuate the beliefs of the winners.

For eons planet Earth has been dominated by people who have been blinded by the illusions of duality. This has led to innumerable dualistic conflicts. Thus, the winner of any conflict has been blinded by the illusions of duality, meaning that they wrote history in such a way that it perpetuates these illusions.

Those who have written history have never been able to see that it is possible to resolve conflicts without war. In fact, many of them have believed that war is the best or the only way to resolve a conflict.

Practitioners of non-war understand that most people have been brought up with a view of history that is distorted in such a way that it prevents them from seeing through the dualistic illusions. People cannot see the basic fact that one can never understand the history of this planet without understanding how the mind of duality has perverted every aspect of human endeavor.

Nor can one understand history without seeing how there has always been an elite whose members have attempted to control the people through ignorance. In many cases the power elite have also used physical force. But behind this overt form of control is the control of people's minds through the illusions of duality. The power elite do not want the dualistic illusions to be exposed. For they need the veil of duality in order to remain hidden from the people.

Practitioners of non-war know that without an understanding of the basic dynamic between the force of peace and the forces of war, one cannot understand history. Thus, one will never see that the real struggle on Earth is the struggle between varying power elite groups and the people, the elite struggling to control the people and the people struggling to be free.

Practitioners of non-war seek to awaken the people to this dynamic, so they no longer have to strive for freedom while wearing blindfolds. Instead of fighting against the elite, the people can draw upon the wisdom and energy of the Infinite. Instead of seeking to destroy the elite, they will make the elite obsolete.

Practitioners of non-war seek to help people see that those who do not learn from the mistakes of history are destined to repeat them. The major mistake of history being a failure to understand the influence of the dualistic mind and the illusion of separation from the Infinite.

Only by using the key of knowledge to draw upon the wisdom of the Infinite from within themselves, will the people escape the control of the elite. By unleashing their infinite potential, the people of Earth can throw off all shackles and become open doors for a Golden Age of non-dual peace and infinite abundance.

Practitioners of non-war have a clear vision and intention that they are here to change the course of history. They are here to neutralize the illusions and consume the energies that support the forces of war. They are here to set this planet on a course that will take it away from war and bring it back into the flow of the River of Life.

The dualistic mind says:

Now an army is exposed to six calamities, not arising from natural causes, but from faults for which the general is responsible. These are: (1) Flight; (2) insubordination; (3) collapse; (4) ruin; (5) disorganization; (6) rout.

The non-dualistic mind says:

The greatest calamity to which any army is exposed is the fact that those participating in the art of war inevitably generate an opposing impulse from the cosmic mirror. This impulse will precipitate material circumstances that will eventually cause the destruction of any army and any nation that is committed to war.

Those who live by the sword will inevitably die by the sword. For when you seek to destroy other people through war, the cosmic mirror can only reason that you want to experience what it is like to be destroyed through war. Due to the law of free will, the mirror must fulfill your wishes.

The dualistic mind says:

Other conditions being equal, if one force is hurled against another ten times its size, the result will be the flight of the former.

The non-dualistic mind says:

Practitioners of non-war base their lives on the rock of the Infinite and are therefore not moved by any finite conditions. They never seek to escape a finite challenge, for they know that the wisdom and energy of the Infinite can overcome any finite condition.

They know that ultimate refuge can never be found in the finite world but only through union with the Infinite.

The dualistic mind says:

When the common soldiers are too strong and their officers too weak, the result is insubordination. When the officers are too strong and the common soldiers too weak, the result is collapse.

The non-dualistic mind says:

Practitioners of non-war do not need rank, for they see that each individual has infinite value. All are united through a common goal and a common vision, allowing those who fill leadership positions to make decisions without risk of insubordination.

The dualistic mind says:

When the higher officers are angry and insubordinate, and on meeting the enemy give battle on their own account from a feeling of resentment, before the commander-in-chief can tell whether or not he is in a position to fight, the result is ruin.

The non-dualistic mind says:

Practitioners of non-war base their decisions on the wisdom of the Infinite instead of finite conditions. Thus, they receive incomparable guidance on how to avoid ruin.

The dualistic mind says:

When the general is weak and without authority; when his orders are not clear and distinct; when there are no fixed duties assigned to officers and men, and the ranks are formed in a slovenly haphazard manner, the result is utter disorganization.

The non-dualistic mind says:

Practitioners of non-war are united through their individual connections to the Infinite. They can often act with no physical connection, yet their efforts serve to further the greater vision and goal of the Infinite.

This is superior organization that is not subject to the finite forces of disorder.

Practitioners of non-war recognize the broader truth in the second law of thermodynamics, namely that in any closed system, disorder must inevitably increase. A closed system is one based on the dualistic mind. This mind always contains at least two opposing forces, and the tension between them will inevitably break down the system.

By uniting with the Infinite, practitioners of non-war raise themselves above the dualistic forces and are no longer subject to the breakdown of order. The *only* way to avoid becoming a closed system is to diligently maintain one's direct connection to the Infinite. The quintessential example of a closed system is the dualistic mind.

The dualistic mind says:

When a general, unable to estimate the enemy's strength, allows an inferior force to engage a larger one, or hurls a weak detachment against a powerful one, and neglects to place picked soldiers in the front rank, the result must be rout.

The non-dualistic mind says:

Practitioners of non-war are not engaged in the dualistic struggle between finite forces, and thus they are not moved by finite conditions. This is the incomparable way to avoid being routed by finite appearances.

The dualistic mind says:

These are six ways of courting defeat, which must be carefully noted by the general who has attained a responsible post.

The non-dualistic mind says:

There is only one sure way to avoid defeat, namely to refrain from engaging in the dualistic struggle. This leads to the incomparable victory of oneness with the Infinite.

The dualistic mind says:

If fighting is sure to result in victory, then you must fight, even though the ruler forbid it; if fighting will not result in victory, then you must not fight even at the ruler's bidding.

The non-dualistic mind says:

The only true ruler is the Infinite. The Infinite will *never* require one extension of itself to fight and kill another.

Instead, it will provide infinite wisdom that leads to unity in the finite world. Fighting will be avoided through the discovery of non-dualistic solutions that dissolve dualistic appearances of conflict.

The dualistic mind says:

The general who advances without coveting fame and retreats without fearing disgrace, whose only thought is to protect his country and do good service for his sovereign, is the jewel of the kingdom.

The non-dualistic mind says:

The true jewel of any nation is the citizens who with steadfast vision, love and determination pursue the non-dualistic cause of their true sovereign—the Infinite. They seek non-violent solutions to every problem.

They will bring the incomparable wisdom and energy of the Infinite into the service of their nation, precipitating the abundant life for all citizens.

The dualistic mind says:

Regard your soldiers as your children, and they will follow you into the deepest valleys; look upon them as your own beloved sons, and they will stand by you even unto death.

The non-dualistic mind says:

That you may be the children of your Father which is the Infinite: for it makes its sun rise on the evil and on the good, and sends rain on the just and on the unjust.

Yet only those who are free from the dualistic illusions will be able to receive the abundant life that is offered freely to all. Many are called, but few are chosen—for few choose to abandon all selfishness and work for raising the All.

The dualistic mind says:

If we know that the enemy is open to attack, but are unaware that our own men are not in a condition to attack, we have gone only halfway towards victory.

The non-dualistic mind says:

Practitioners of non-war go the whole way toward victory by studying and removing the beam in their own eye, namely the dualistic mind and the separate self that spring from the illusion of separation.

Having done so, they see clearly how to help other people remove the separate self from *their* minds. This is going the whole way towards incomparable victory.

The dualistic mind says:

If we know that the enemy is open to attack, and also know that our men are in a condition to attack, but are unaware that the nature of the ground makes fighting impracticable, we have still gone only halfway towards victory.

The non-dualistic mind says:

Practitioners of non-war go the whole way towards victory by studying how every aspect of life on Earth has been influenced and distorted by dualistic illusions. Having removed those illusions from their own minds, they now set out to help others do the same. This leads to incomparable victory for the individual and for the planet as a whole.

The dualistic mind says:

The experienced soldier, once in motion, is never bewildered; once he has broken camp, he is never at a loss.

Hence the saying: If you know the enemy and know yourself, your victory will not stand in doubt; if you know Heaven and know Earth, you may make your victory complete.

The non-dualistic mind says:

Practitioners of non-war are never bewildered, for they have direct access to the wisdom of the Infinite.

Being awakened to reality, they see the Infinite within themselves. Having attained non-dualistic vision, they see the Infinite within all other people. Thus, they truly know themselves, and they truly know others.

Having attained non-dualistic vision, practitioners of non-war see the Infinite behind all finite appearances. Thus, they truly know Heaven, and they truly know Earth.

This leads to a truly complete victory, the incomparable victory that is not aimed at defeating a finite enemy but seeks the growth of the entire Body of the Infinite. This is the victory whereby all extensions of the Infinite return to the Infinite through their finite journey.

Chapter 11.
Non-dual Situations

The dualistic mind says:

The art of war recognizes nine varieties of ground: (1) Dispersive ground; (2) Facile ground; (3) Contentious ground; (4) Open ground; (5) Ground of intersecting highways; (6) Serious ground; (7) Difficult ground; (8) Hemmed-in ground; (9) Desperate ground.

The non-dualistic mind says:

The art of non-war recognizes many ways to approach others for the sake of awakening them to the reality of the Infinite. Practitioners of non-war know that when they approach others, they will find that people belong to one of the following categories:

- People who are open to a higher understanding. These people might have a natural desire to understand more about life or a particular aspect of life. Or they might face a difficult situation and they are open to a better way of dealing with it.

- People who are indifferent. These people have closed their minds to a higher understanding. Some are so focused on enjoying the material universe that they don't care about a higher understanding, others have been trapped in the illusion that there is no such understanding. They want to live their lives the way they have always done. They do not want to be disturbed by anything, even if it could lead to greater spiritual and material abundance.

- People who are hostile. Some people think they have already found the ultimate understanding or belief system, and thus there could not possibly be anything higher. They have elevated a finite expression of truth to a graven image and think anything that goes beyond their mental box is a threat. Such people are often driven by a combination of fear and pride, a blend of the inferiority and superiority complexes. They feel their finite expression of truth is superior to all other finite expressions, yet they also feel their expression is constantly under threat. They will often respond with hostility to anyone who seeks to expand their understanding.

Practitioners of non-war recognize that each group must be approached in different ways. This is how to approach people who are open-minded:

1. Do not *preach* your truth but *live* it. Those who seek to preach an expression of truth that is understood only intellectually, end up in dualistic battles with others who have likewise understood their expression of truth only with the intellect. This will lead to emotional tension, possibly physical conflict, and thus the cause of the Infinite is not advanced. On the contrary, the dualistic mind is strengthened and the forces of war know how to take advantage of such people.

Practitioners of non-war seek first a direct experience of the kingdom of the Infinite and the right use of their creative faculties. They seek to internalize their expression of truth to the point where they have transcended the outer expression and attained a direct connection with the Infinite within themselves. When living their truth, expressing it in all situations, they will find that other people will spontaneously ask them why they are always at peace. This is the most advantageous way to approach others, for those who ask spontaneously are open to a higher understanding.

2. Share your truth. Having internalized your truth, be open to sharing it spontaneously. Do not seek to evaluate with the intellect when and how to share your truth. Instead, be open to letting your infinite self share that truth through you at any time. Allow the words of your infinite self to flow through you rather than seeking to design words with the finite mind. You will find that your infinite self knows exactly what to say in order to help another person open his or her mind to a higher understanding of some aspect of life. You are not seeking to get others to accept the ideas you present with their outer minds. You are seeking to help others connect to their infinite selves, so they can get inner confirmation that what you say is true.

3. Ask questions. Be open to letting your infinite self ask expansive questions through you. Do not let your outer mind formulate the questions, for it will only lead to a battle of intellects or

questions that are colored by lower emotions, such as fear of rejection, irony, sarcasm or aggressive suggestion. Dualistic questions seek to tear down another person's belief system or even destroy the person's faith in anything. Instead, let your infinite self ask the exact question that will open the mind of another person to something beyond his or her present understanding.

4. Make expansive suggestions. Respect the free will of others and never tell them what to believe or how to live their lives. Do not seek to tear down the beliefs of other people but seek only to expand their understanding. Destroying other people's belief systems will not awaken them to the reality of the Infinite. It will leave them in a vacuum that is either filled by another dualistic belief system or causing them to doubt everything.

Darkness cannot be removed from a room, so do not fall prey to the temptation to battle against all finite belief systems—you could not possibly succeed in a lifetime. Instead, focus on bringing the wisdom of the Infinite and allow your infinite self to make suggestions through you. Such suggestions will often be formulated as a question: "You know there is a non-dualistic way to look at that issue, don't you?" "Do you know that there is a non-dualistic response to that problem?" or "If there was a way to avoid having to struggle like that, would you want to know about it?"

In approaching people who are indifferent, all of the above situations are valid and will awaken some people. Yet many are so trapped in illusions that a more direct approach is necessary in order to help them see the reality that there is an alternative to their current way of life:

1. Probing questions. Be open to allowing your infinite self to ask probing questions through you. These are questions aimed at making people think about and question the limits of their existing beliefs. Such questions do not seek to tear down people's beliefs but seek to help them see that there is more to understand than what is contained in their current mental box. They do not leave people with no beliefs but point to a higher understanding.

2. Point out unanswered questions. Let your infinite self point out the questions that cannot be answered by people's current belief system. You must remain non-attached to how people respond or do not respond.

3. Point out inconsistencies. Let your infinite self point out inconsistencies in people's current beliefs. Take care to let this come from your infinite self and do not let your mental or emotional bodies color it with any form of duality.

4. State a challenging truth. Let your infinite self state a challenging truth through you. Again, do not let this be colored by intellectual reasoning or let it be charged by lower emotions. Remain non-attached to people's reactions so that you are always at peace.

5. Appeal to understanding. Let your infinite self appeal to understanding by explaining that all human progress has been achieved when people dared to think outside their mental boxes and set sail for new horizons. Let your infinite self question why people have to follow the crowd and do what is "normal." If everyone had insisted on continuing to do the same thing, how could there have been progress in society?

6. Give a demonstration. Let your infinite self display a demonstration of a higher truth or a better way to live. Dare to be a person who does not follow the crowd. Show others that there is a better way to live, a way that leads to greater peace and joy.

In approaching people who are hostile, be alert against the temptation to be drawn into their dualistic state of mind. Practitioners of non-war understand that people are hostile because they are always feeling threatened. They are subconsciously demanding that other people respond in one of two ways:

- Submit to them and acknowledge that their belief system is the only true one and that they are superior to you.

- Take the position of an enemy and oppose them and their belief system.

Practitioners of non-war understand that these two reactions represent the two opposite dualistic extremes. If you respond in either way, you only confirm hostile people's dualistic belief system, and thereby you lose any opportunity to shake them out of duality.

In responding to them, find the middle way between the two dualistic extremes. Only by responding in a way that hostile people do not expect, and have not seen before, is there any possibility of opening their minds to a higher understanding.

Practitioners of non-war understand that when dealing with hostile people, it is necessary to be mindful of the law of free will. This means not seeking to force these people's will, but it also means not expecting particular results. Even some of the greatest spiritual teachers of history have been rejected by closed-minded people. Jesus was rejected by the scribes, the Pharisees, the lawyers and the temple priests and the Buddha was rejected by the Brahmins.

Be mindful not to let hostile people violate *your* free will and cause you to hold back your truth. If you find that dealing with such people disturbs your peace and takes away your joy, then withdraw temporarily and look for the beam in your own eye that makes you vulnerable. For only when the prince of this world has nothing in you – whereby he can cause a non-peaceful reaction – can you deal with hostile people and still be yourself.

Practitioners of non-war see hostile people as a test for themselves, a test in how well they can maintain their peace. If you find that such people disturb your peace, then take it as an opportunity to look for and remove the elements of non-peace in your own mind. See every situation as an opportunity for you to grow ever closer to the incomparable peace of union with the Infinite. Let go of anything that keeps you from that peace.

When you are fully united with the Infinite, no finite conditions can take away your peace. This is true freedom in which other people and material conditions have no power over you

***

Practitioners of non-war understand that no finite expression of truth is the actual truth. Truth is the Spirit of the Infinite, and it can be experienced only by reaching beyond any finite expression. They also understand that hostile people do not see this fact, and thus they have elevated their expression of truth to the status of infallibility.

Practitioners of non-war understand that the intellect can reason for or against any idea. By using the intellect, any belief system can be raised to the status of infallibility. Once people believe in such a graven image, they can use the intellect to refute any argument you could possibly mount against their belief system.

Practitioners of war often engage in endless intellectual quarrels, because they believe it is possible to mount a final intellectual argument. Many of these people would never resort to physical violence or force and think they are peaceful people. Yet they are still engaged in the dualistic struggle by using their intellects to combat the ideas held by other people.

Such people may think they are working for peace, but in reality their minds are feeding the forces of war. Practitioners of non-war know that there is no finite or absolute argument that can be expressed in words. Thus, they avoid being pulled into the never-ending struggle for intellectual superiority.

The ultimate argument is a direct, inner experience of the reality of the Infinite. Only when one experiences the reality of the Infinite, will one see that all finite arguments are in the realm of duality and are ultimately unreal or incomplete.

Experience supersedes all finite arguments. When people are not open to such a direct experience, they are unreachable for any higher truth.

Because practitioners of non-war understand this fact, they can avoid being pulled into dualistic conflicts with hostile people. These are some of the ways to approach hostile people, yet practitioners of non-war know that there is no sure way to awaken those who have closed their minds with the double lock of fear and pride:

1. Do not engage; wait for them to engage you. Do not formulate an intent to prove hostile people wrong, to open their minds or to convert them. Focus on living and demonstrating your truth. In doing so, you will inevitably threaten hostile people's belief system, and this will cause them to attack you. You can then demonstrate how to respond in a non-dualistic manner.

2. Do not be moved. Hostile people are hostile because they are trapped in duality. When your belief system is based on the shifting sands of duality, it can be threatened and thus people are engaged in an ongoing struggle to defend what cannot be defended. This causes them to – often subconsciously – attempt to draw you into the dualistic struggle. One way to do this is to get you to submit. This, means that you either accept their belief system and join them or that you are so intimidated by their hostility that you remain silent. Practitioners of non-war see

through this mechanism and remain unmoved, continuing to express their non-dualistic truth.

3. Do not fight back. If you will not join them or be intimidated into silence, hostile people will seek to get you to fight back. This will allow them to label you as an enemy, and they can now feel justified in seeking to destroy your belief system. If that does not work, they feel justified in seeking to destroy you. Practitioners of non-war see through this mechanism and refuse to fight back. They will neither fight nor take flight.

When you know who you are as an extension of the Infinite, you can never feel attacked by other people. When you do not feel attacked, there is no need to defend yourself by attacking others. This is turning the other cheek.

When you cannot withdraw and cannot fight back, then what is left? Practitioners of non-war have been awakened from the illusions of duality, which say that you have to respond by going into one of the dualistic extremes. They look beyond all dualistic responses and seek first union with the Infinite. Through this union, they can draw upon the wisdom of the Infinite, which can find a non-dualistic response to every situation. The Infinite has an infinite number of non-dualistic responses, yet these are a few of the possibilities:

1. Ask challenging questions. Any dualistic belief system is based on a partial understanding of the issue Thus, it is always possible to ask questions that the system cannot answer. This can demonstrate the limitations of the system and the need to reach for a higher understand-

ing from beyond the finite world. Some people will respond to this.

2. State a truth. Instead of seeking to prove hostile people or their arguments wrong, simply state a higher truth and keep doing so without directly engaging in the dualistic arguments. Some will come to see that there is something beyond their present beliefs.

3. Point out inconsistencies. Any dualistic belief system will, by its nature, have built-in contradictions. When these are pointed out, some people can be awakened.

4. Point out the limitations of duality. Many hostile people cannot see beyond the dualistic mind and have never considered its limitations. Some can be awakened by being shown the difference between duality and non-duality. However, they will need to see you demonstrate – often many times – a non-dualistic response to their dualistic attacks.

5. Point to a better way. People cannot exist in a vacuum, so if you seek to break down hostile people's beliefs, they will only feel more threatened. Instead, seek to point to advantages of adopting a non-dualistic approach to life. Demonstrate those advantages instead of just talking about them.

6. Turn the other cheek. When met with great hostility, always remain at peace. In some cases, allow other people to abuse you. For only when they see that they cannot take away your peace,

will they realize that you have something they do not have.

7. Make evil visible. This can be done by pointing out that the beliefs or actions of others do not live up to a universal standard (including their own professed belief system) or that they lead to consequences that have not been seen or acknowledged. Yet in some cases it can be necessary to let others abuse you in order to finally make their evil so visible that some will see it.

8. Be the judgment. Some people are so trapped in fear or pride that they will do almost anything to destroy what they see as a threat. In some cases, practitioners of non-war must be willing to serve as the instrument for the judgment of such people, so that they can be removed from the Earth. This is done by making the sacrifice of letting others abuse you so they bring about their own judgment.

Practitioners of non-war do not decide how to respond with the outer, analytical mind. They always let their responses be guided by the wisdom of the Infinite. They recognize that they can of their own selves do nothing, but that it is the infinite self who is the true doer.

In this way practitioners of non-war can overcome the greatest temptation that hostile people represent, namely the temptation to see them as opponents or enemies. Practitioners of non-war see themselves as extensions of the Infinite, and thus they see all other people as extensions of the Infinite.

Hostile people are not enemies. They are potential allies who are only temporarily blinded by the illusions of duality that spring from the greater illusion of separation. If they can be helped to overcome that illusion, unity can be achieved and thus more abundance can be precipitated by the combination of minds.

Practitioners of non-war know that the Infinite has no desire to condemn or punish anyone. They make themselves instruments for the Infinite to exercise its desire to awaken all people from the illusions of duality. They work to help all people inherit the abundant life that it is the Infinite's good pleasure to give them.

Practitioners of non-war have no opinions and make no judgments about other people, no matter how hostile they are. They follow the timeless call to love your enemies, bless them that curse you, do good to them that hate you, and seek to awaken those which despitefully use you and persecute you.

Practitioners of non-war hold the highest vision for other people's awakening, while allowing them complete freedom to exercise their free will. In thus setting other people free, practitioners of non-war also set themselves free from the most subtle temptations to engage in the dualistic struggle. Only in remaining free, can practitioners of non-war make a contribution to the advancement of the cause of the Infinite.

The dualistic mind says:

Those who were called skillful leaders of old knew how to drive a wedge between the enemy's front and rear; to prevent cooperation between his large and small divisions; to hinder the good

troops from rescuing the bad, the officers from rallying their men.

The non-dualistic mind says:

What bondage it is to always be engaged in the dualistic struggle and seek to subdue an enemy while seeking to avoid being subdued. What freedom it is to rise above this and find the incomparable peace of the Infinite.

Practitioners of non-war do not seek to divide other people amongst themselves. They seek to help other people overcome the division between themselves and the Infinite, so that all people can be raised up. Thereby, they seek to turn an opponent into an ally so that all may experience a more abundant life.

The dualistic mind says:

When it was to their advantage, they made a forward move; when otherwise, they stopped still.

The non-dualistic mind says:

What bondage it is to always be engaged in the dualistic struggle to seek a finite advantage and avoid a finite disadvantage. What freedom it is to rise above this and find the incomparable advantage of the Infinite.

The dualistic mind says:

If asked how to cope with a great host of the enemy in orderly array and on the point of marching to the attack, I should say: "Begin by seizing

something which your opponent holds dear; then he will be amenable to your will."

The non-dualistic mind says:

What bondage it is to always be engaged in the dualistic struggle to take something from others and make them subject to your will. What freedom it is to rise above this to find the incomparable peace of the Infinite. This leads to union with the greater will of one's own infinite being.

The dualistic mind says:

Carefully study the well-being of your men, and do not overtax them. Concentrate your energy and hoard your strength. Keep your army continually on the move, and devise unfathomable plans.

The non-dualistic mind says:

Seek the ultimate well-being of all people associated with you in always working to help them expand their connection to the Infinite. Yet also be aware of how to help them experience greater well-being in the material world.

Practitioners of non-war see the Infinite within themselves. They see that everything in the material universe is simply the energy of the Infinite that has taken on a finite disguise. They honor the material world as an expression of the Infinite and seek to bring the abundance of the Infinite into greater expression in the finite. Thus, they polish both sides of the coin of life.

Practitioners of non-war keep their company continually moving closer to the Infinite. They let their plans spring spontaneously from the wisdom of the Infinite, thus making them unfathomable to those trapped in the dualistic mind.

The dualistic mind says:

Throw your soldiers into positions whence there is no escape, and they will prefer death to flight. If they will face death, there is nothing they may not achieve. Officers and men alike will put forth their uttermost strength.

The non-dualistic mind says:

What folly that one should have to force people to face death in order to get them to put forth their best in a finite battle against a finite enemy, a battle that could have no real consequence. What folly that people should be faced with "kill or be killed" as their only options. Surely, there is always an alternative to such dualistic blindness.

Better to help people face the reality of the Infinite, which gives them a true motivation of knowing they are working for a non-dualistic cause. By seeking to help people attain a direct inner connection to the Infinite, they will be able to achieve all things, for they will spontaneously put forth their uttermost strength—the incomparable strength of the Infinite within them.

The dualistic mind says:

Soldiers when in desperate straits lose the sense of fear. If there is no place of refuge, they

will stand firm. If they are in hostile country, they will show a stubborn front. If there is no help for it, they will fight hard.

The non-dualistic mind says:

Far better to help people achieve oneness with the Infinite, which is the *only* way to fully escape fear. Only those who have found the ultimate refuge of union with the Infinite, can truly stand firm against all finite conditions.

The dualistic mind says:

Thus, without waiting to be marshaled, the soldiers will be constantly on the alert; without waiting to be asked, they will do your will; without restrictions, they will be faithful; without giving orders, they can be trusted.

The non-dualistic mind says:

Far better to help people attain union with the Infinite, so that all can move spontaneously in pursuit of the cause of the Infinite, which is to set all people free from the illusions of duality. Such people will spontaneously be faithful and trustworthy, for they are unmoved by any finite conditions.

The dualistic mind says:

Prohibit the taking of omens, and do away with superstitious doubts. Then, until death itself comes, no calamity need be feared.

The non-dualistic mind says:

All superstitious thoughts are dualistic thoughts; all thoughts that spring from duality are superstitious. The *only* way to overcome superstition is to connect to the wisdom of the Infinite.

Fear is the inevitable companion of the illusion of separation. Once you are separated from the River of Life, death becomes a possibility. A sense of identity that is based on separation from the Infinite cannot exist indefinitely. Thus, only by overcoming the illusion of separation can one eliminate the cause of fear.

In so doing, one will also rise above the fear of death, even above death itself. For through union with the Infinite, even the last enemy will be conquered.

The dualistic mind says:

The principle on which to manage an army is to set up one standard of courage which all must reach.

The non-dualistic mind says:

Practitioners of non-war know that the ultimate standard for any human being is to be the open door for the power, wisdom and love of the Infinite. This leads to the incomparable courage that is based on union with the Infinite. Nothing less will lead to inner or outer peace.

The dualistic mind says:

It is the business of a general to be quiet and thus ensure secrecy; upright and just, and thus maintain order.

He must be able to mystify his officers and men by false reports and appearances, and thus keep them in total ignorance.

The non-dualistic mind says:

Practitioners of non-war have no need to keep other people in ignorance or to mystify them. They know that ultimate order can be attained only through ultimate knowledge, which can be attained only through union with the wisdom of the Infinite. Thus, they seek to help others escape ignorance by attaining a direct, inner connection to the Infinite.

Yet those who let their plans flow spontaneously from the wisdom of the Infinite, may indeed mystify those who have not yet achieved their own inner connection.

The dualistic mind says:

By altering his arrangements and changing his plans, he keeps the enemy without definite knowledge. By shifting his camp and taking circuitous routes, he prevents the enemy from anticipating his purpose.

The non-dualistic mind says:

Practitioners of non-war seek first union with the Infinite. When union is achieved, they have no need for plans, for they let their actions flow spontaneously from the wisdom of the Infinite. Thus, no mind blinded by duality can ever anticipate their purpose or predict their actions.

The dualistic mind says:

We cannot enter into alliance with neighboring princes until we are acquainted with their designs.

The non-dualistic mind says:

True alliances can be attained only when all participants have achieved at least some inner connection to the Infinite. True alliances are based on trust, and only people who have achieved complete union with the Infinite are ultimately trustworthy.

The dualistic mind says:

Place your army in deadly peril, and it will survive; plunge it into desperate straits, and it will come off in safety.

The non-dualistic mind says:

Practitioners of non-war know that ultimate safety and survival can be achieved only through union with the Infinite. Thus, they do not spend their energy and attention on seeking the safety and survival of their separate selves. Rather, they are willing to lose their separate selves in order to attain the incomparable life of union with the Infinite.

Practitioners of war think some finite advantage represents an ultimate prize for which they are willing to risk their lives. Practitioners of non-war know that the pearl of great price is union with the Infinite. Thus, they are willing to let go of all their finite "possessions" and attachments in order to secure the one incomparable pearl.

The dualistic mind says:

Success in warfare is gained by carefully accommodating ourselves to the enemy's purpose.

The non-dualistic mind says:

Success in the art of non-war is gained by carefully accommodating oneself to the purpose of the Infinite.

Chapter 12.
The Use of Spiritual Fire

The dualistic mind says:

There are five ways of attacking with fire. The first is to burn soldiers in their camp; the second is to burn stores; the third is to burn baggage trains; the fourth is to burn arsenals and magazines; the fifth is to hurl dropping fire amongst the enemy.

The non-dualistic mind says:

What folly to spend one's energy and attention on learning how to destroy other people. Truly, only the complete spiritual blindness of the dualistic mind can cause one, expression of the Infinite to contemplate how to destroy another expression of the Infinite. Surely, those who contemplate how to kill with fire must themselves die by fire.

Practitioners of non-war have no desire to destroy others by using physical fire—or any other means. Yet they know the value of spiritual fire.

Practitioners of non-war know that there are no absolute or final arguments in the finite world. Any intellectual argument can be counteracted by another intellectual argument. Any statement expressed in words can be gainsaid by another statement expressed in words. This explains why so many people in the modern world are trapped in a state of mind in which they think nothing is real or that there is no ultimate truth.

There is no way to awaken others by using only intellectual arguments or statements expressed in words. To fully awaken others, it is necessary to bring the energy – the spiritual fire – of the Infinite. For only when people experience this fire, will they be infused with Life. The fire of the Infinite is like the sun that dispels the mist of duality.

Practitioners of non-war seek not only to become open doors for the wisdom of the Infinite; they seek likewise to become open doors for the fire of the Infinite. This fire will burn through the walls that people have erected around their minds. It will penetrate through all of people's mental defenses and emotional blockages.

The spiritual fire of the Infinite will burn through the hardened shell and reach the very heart of the person. It will thus stir the person's inner longing for something more, the inner longing for the Infinite.

Only when the inner longing is stirred – with such intensity that the outer mind of the person recognizes the longing – will the person be moved to look beyond his or her mental box in order to satisfy the longing for a more abundant life.

Only when people feel the resonance between the fire of the Infinite and something in themselves, will they be awakened to the reality of the Infinite. For the Infinite has written its laws in people's inward parts – their higher minds – but the lower mind has forgotten this law. Thus, a measure of spiritual fire is needed in order to awaken people to the reality that they are more than human beings—they are spiritual beings in a human body.

Practitioners of war are well aware of the existence and value of spiritual fire, and they often seek to take it by force so as to use it for their selfish purposes. Yet this cannot be done, for one who has selfish motives can never reach the fire of the Infinite. However, such a one can reach an energy that is not of the spiritual realm yet is not physical. This energy comes from the lower spirits in the mental and emotional realms, the spirits that make up the non-material parts of the forces of war.

Such non-spiritual fire can indeed empower people and even help them produce signs and wonders. Yet the price to pay is high. For the prince of this world will promise you that you will rule all the kingdoms of this world—but only if you give him your soul.

Practitioners of non-war know that although the prince of this world makes sweeping promises, they cannot be fulfilled. For the opposing forces of duality will prevent any finite person or force from ruling all the kingdoms of this world.

Practitioners of non-war also know that it will never profit them to gain the whole world but lose their souls. Thus, they seek no reward in the finite world but seek the incomparable reward of union with the Infinite.

***

In becoming an open door for the fire of the Infinite, one must never seek to control this fire, for spiritual fire can never be controlled by a being in the finite world. One must be open to letting the winds of the Spirit blow where they listeth.

Only those who have attained total and unconditional surrender of the separate self can flow with the winds of the

Spirit, with the River of Life. Complete surrender of the illusion of a separate self is the condition for complete union with the Infinite.

The only force that can burn away the separate self is the fire of the Infinite, yet the fire will not violate people's free will. Thus, as long as people hold on to the "life' of the separate self, they cannot be ultimately free. One must be willing to lose this false sense of life in order to have the fire of the Infinite burn away the separate self.

One must become the open door for the fire to burn away one's own separate self, and then one will become the open door for the fire to burn away the separate selves of others according to their free will. For the Infinite truly is a consuming fire that consumes all unlike itself.

Practitioners of non-war have the courage – the total courage that comes from total surrender of the separate self – to face the trial by fire. They let their work be tried by the fire of the Infinite, lovingly letting go of all that is burned while joyfully accepting all that burns with fire but is not consumed.

Practitioners of non-war know that they can increase the flow of spiritual fire through them by using appropriate techniques for invoking this fire. Such techniques are found in many spiritual traditions and new techniques are occasionally released by the force of peace.*

Practitioners of non-war know that spiritual fire is the only factor that can consume the low-frequency energies that make it difficult for people to rise above the downward pull of the dualistic mind and the forces of war.

* To find techniques released for people in modern times, see *www.askrealjesus.com* and *www.mothermarysgarden.com*.

They start by invoking fire to free themselves. Then they invoke fire to awaken others. Next, they invoke fire to free their nations, and finally they invoke fire to clear the collective consciousness and free the entire planet.

The dualistic mind says:

A kingdom that has once been destroyed can never come again into being; nor can the dead ever be brought back to life.

Hence the enlightened ruler is heedful, and the good general full of caution. This is the way to keep a country at peace and an army intact.

The non-dualistic mind says:

Finite forces can never resurrect a destroyed kingdom or bring the dead back to life. For their internal divisions and conflicts can only break down and destroy.

Yet through union with the Infinite even paradise lost can be restored. Thus, planet Earth can indeed be restored to its former state of purity and abundance. Practitioners of non-war hold the vision of a Golden Age for the Earth, an age in which permanent peace and never-ending abundance will be manifest on Earth.

They do not await the coming of an external savior but allow the Infinite to be reborn in their hearts. For they know that the second coming of the Infinite is the coming of the Infinite in themselves. And only when a critical mass of people allow the Infinite to come again in themselves, will the second coming – the awakening – occur on a planetary scale and a Golden Age be manifest.

Chapter 13.
Non-dualistic Foreknowledge

The dualistic mind says:

Thus, what enables the wise sovereign and the good general to strike and conquer, and achieve things beyond the reach of ordinary men, is foreknowledge.

Now this foreknowledge cannot be elicited from spirits; it cannot be obtained inductively from experience, nor by any deductive calculation.

Knowledge of the enemy's dispositions can only be obtained from other men.

The non-dualistic mind says:

Practitioners of non-war, having been awakened from the illusions of duality, have overcome fear. Fear is the driving force behind wanting foreknowledge, for fear gives people the desire to have a guarantee of success before starting any endeavor.

Practitioners of non-war are connected to the Infinite and thus have unwavering trust in the Infinite. They approach every situation as an opportunity to learn how to express their creative faculties. And since every situation gives one the opportunity to learn what works and what does not work, what then is the need for foreknowledge?

Practitioners of non-war do not seek foreknowledge from lower spirits or from material means of prediction. Nor do they rely on induction or deduction. Yet neither do they rely on knowledge from other people, even though they listen to others.

Practitioners of non-war seek first to maintain their connection and unity with the Infinite. Thereby, they will spontaneously do the right thing without knowing beforehand what to do or what the outcome will be. They know that they do not need to have conscious foreknowledge when they have access to the knowledge of the Infinite, the knowledge that spans past, present and future.

The dualistic mind says:

Hence it is only the enlightened ruler and the wise general who will use the highest intelligence of the army for purposes of spying and thereby they achieve great results. Spies are a most important element in war, because on them depends an army's ability to move.

The non-dualistic mind says:

What freedom to rise above the need to spy on others. What peace comes from knowing that one's actions are based on the wisdom of the Infinite and will therefore lead to incomparable success.

What freedom to have no demands or expectations. One acts upon inner direction and then watches in wonder as the Infinite unfolds the abundant life in one's world.

Chapter 14.
Knowing Duality and Non-duality

Nothing is more important for practitioners of non-war than to discern between the non-dual reality of the Infinite and the innumerable illusions of the dualistic mind. On this topic the dualistic mind has nothing to say, for how could this mind ever be both wise as a serpent and harmless as a dove? How could it ever see its own unreality? Thus, the non-dualistic mind will speak.

Practitioners of non-war are willing to look at and remove the beam in their own eye, and they are willing to look for elements of duality in their consciousness on an ongoing basis. For they know that as long as their sense of self is centered in the muddied energy field of Earth, the subtle illusions and low-frequency energies of duality may find inroads into their container of self. Constant vigilance is the price for being a practitioner of non-war.

Practitioners of non-war see that, in recorded history, there has not been a time when the opportunity to remove the beam from one's own eye has been greater. That is because today's people have so much knowledge of the human psyche, knowledge that was not available in past ages.

Through the fields of psychology, self-help and universal spirituality, much knowledge has been brought forth about the nature of the human ego. This ego – when understood as a separate self based on an inherent conflict – is what Jesus called the beam in your own eye and what the Buddha called the cause of attachments and thus the origin of human suffering.

Practitioners of non-war study the psyche and the ego from all available perspectives. They do this first of all to overcome the gravitational pull of their own egos, for they realize that until they clear their own minds, they cannot possibly see clearly how to help other people or improve the world.

Once they have learned how to see through and surrender the illusions of their own egos, they use their newfound vision to help others. They also point out how the human ego has influenced every aspect of society. For truly, every problem in human history can be traced back to the spiritual blindness of the ego.

What then is the primary effect of the ego? It is that it keeps you – the conscious self – separated from the Infinite by keeping you trapped in the illusions of duality. The separation from the Infinite is not a real separation, for nothing can be truly separated from the Infinite that is everywhere present.

Yet once you have used your free will to accept the illusion of separation, you will project images of separation into the cosmic mirror. And what can the mirror do but send back material circumstances that reflect – and thus seem to confirm – your belief in separation? Even the current density of physical matter seems to confirm the illusion that the material world is separated from the Infinite or that the Infinite does not exist.

***

There are many who are waiting for some supernatural event – such as the second coming of some prophet or leader from the past – to give humans undeniable proof that the Infinite is real. Yet practitioners of non-war understand that this would be a violation of free will. Plausible deniability of the existence of the Infinite is necessary in order to let free will outplay itself. Thus, they no longer look for an external savior but seek to enter the kingdom within them. They know that although the Infinite is everywhere, you will never find it as long as you are looking for it outside yourself.

Practitioners of non-war understand that before they can see the Infinite within themselves, they must overcome the ego. This is the separate self that can survive only by preventing you from seeing the Infinite within yourself. The ego must prevent you from recognizing and accepting yourself as an extension of the Infinite, an individualization of the Infinite. For when you attain full self-knowledge, you will know that when the ego dies, *you* will not die. Thus, you can surrender the ego into the all-consuming fire of the Infinite. Those who do not have this knowledge are afraid to look at, let alone surrender, their egos. For they fear that if the ego dies, they will die also.

The ego is based on the illusion of separation, which means that the very fabric of the ego is the belief that your individuality must of necessity be a separate being. The ego can never fathom that you could have individuality while still remaining one with the Infinite out of which you were born. The ego can never fathom the mystery that because the Infinite is everywhere, it cannot be divided and thus no separation is possible. Therefore, individual beings are not like separate water drops. They are like waves that rise out of the ocean but are still one with the ocean.

The ego believes that the very fact that you have self-awareness as an individual being means that you have separated from the ocean. The ego believes that when you claimed your individuality, you were expelled from paradise and that you will never be allowed to return unless you give up your individuality.

The ego will never understand that it was not your individuality that caused you to leave paradise behind. "Paradise" is a synonym for a state of consciousness in which you know that you are an individual being but still an extension of the Infinite and thus one with the Infinite. This is the state of mind in which you walk and talk with the Infinite – and its representatives in the force of peace – in the Garden of Life.

This state of innocence allows you to journey into the world of form – even the density of the material universe – without losing your awareness of who you are and from where you came. Thus, you can have dominion over the Earth, meaning that you can express your creativity on Earth without being blinded by the illusions of duality that have polluted the energy field of this planet and the collective consciousness of humankind.

You can be *in* the world, yet not *of* the world. You can have dominion over the Earth instead of allowing the Earth – as a symbol for the density of the duality consciousness – to have dominion over your sense of self.

The loss of this state of oneness – this state of innocence or grace – was not due to the punishment of an angry God. It was due to an act of free will on your part. You made this choice because you had become blinded by the illusions and temptations of the dualistic mind. Yet you were the one who allowed those illusions to enter, and thus you are the only one who can expel them from the sacred temple of your being. You were the one who came to see them as real, and you are the one who must come to see them as unreal.

***

Practitioners of non-war have taken full responsibility for themselves. They acknowledge that the loss of the consciousness of oneness was due to a decision they made. They accept that they can regain oneness only through their own decisions. Thus, they have taken back their power to change their lives instead of giving that power to the ego, other people or the forces of war.

Following this mystical path back to union with the Infinite – the middle way of the Buddha and the straight and narrow way of Christ – requires three elements:

- Removing the lower energies of duality from one's energy field. The key to doing this is to invoke the high-frequency energy of the Infinite in order to transform the low-frequency energy of duality. This also empowers one to transform energy impulses from the past before they become manifest as physical circumstances. Techniques for doing this have been and are being released by the force of peace.

- Seeing through the illusions of duality that have entered one's mind, then replacing them with the reality of the Infinite. The key is to draw upon the incomparable – thus non-dualistic – wisdom of the Infinite, which can expose and consume all dualistic illusions. Teachings for helping people start this process have been and are being released by the force of peace.

- Seeing through and then surrendering the separate self, the separate sense of identity, the ego. This is not a matter of transforming the ego but of realizing that it never had any life in it. Only the being that descended from the Infinite – meaning your conscious self – can return to the Infinite. The separate self cannot be resurrected, it cannot be saved. It must be allowed to die in an act of total, unconditional surrender to one's own infinite Being.

Practitioners of non-war use suitable outer teachings and practical tools in order to walk this path. Yet they know that outer tools and teachings will not do all the work for them. In the end, walking the true path is not a mechanical or automatic process. It is a creative process that requires them to attain new insights and make non-dualistic decisions.

Practitioners of non-war do not see themselves as assembly workers who are following a predefined plan for putting together the perfect human being. They see themselves as artists who are venturing into new territory in carving out their true identity—not from the rock of the Earth but from the "rock" of the Infinite.

***

The Infinite is infinite. The finite mind of the separate self and the conscious mind tied to the physical brain cannot fathom the nature of infinity. Yet those who are willing to stretch the mind can glimpse the Infinite behind finite words.

There can be no boundaries in infinity. The Infinite is everywhere and nowhere at the same time, for the Infinite is beyond space and time. There can be no divisions in infinity, and thus there can be no separation. How can anything be separated from the Infinite, when the Infinite is everywhere present?

Separation is possible only for beings who have self-awareness and free will. They can choose to create the *illusion* that they are separated from the Infinite. And the more they believe in the illusion, the more real it will seem.

The inhabitants of a cosmic unit, such as planet Earth, combine their individual minds to form a collective mind. They can collectively create an illusion of separation – a separate collective self – that is so strong that it can overpower the individual minds of most people. Thus, most inhabitants of Earth have grown up believing in the collective illusion that they are separated from the Infinite, either because they are sinners, animals with no spirit or otherwise deficient.

Once such a collective illusion has been formed, it becomes a self-reinforcing downward spiral, a self-fulfilling prophecy. As people become blinded by the illusion of separation, they create more and more dualistic mental images. They also generate more and more lower energy based on fear, anger and other selfish emotions. This energy accumulates in the electronic belt around their planet, and as it pulls on the mental and emotional minds of the people, the illusions of duality seem more and more real.

As they come to believe in the illusion of separation, the inhabitants of a planet formulate mental images based on duality, and they send those images into the cosmic mirror, charged with the force of their limiting emotions. The mirror can do nothing but reflect back material conditions that outpicture the images in the collective mind.

The people are subconsciously saying that they want to experience a state of being separated from the abundant life of the Infinite; they want to experience lack and suffering; they want to experience life as a struggle. The cosmic mirror must comply and give the people what they ask for—until they start asking for something else.

It is possible that the inhabitants of a planet can precipitate material conditions that make it very difficult to see that their world was created by the Infinite. Even matter itself can become so dense that it hides the fact that everything is created from the energy of the Infinite and thus nothing is truly separated from the Infinite. The conditions of lack and suffering make it seem like the Infinite has left the people behind, that the Infinite has lost its power or is no longer willing to work on their planet.

Because the people are blinded by the many dualistic illusions, they cannot see and will not admit that their suffering is not due to the punishment or absence of an external God. It is an entirely self-created condition that is due to the fact that they have created an artificial separation between themselves and the Infinite, a separation that exists only in their own minds.

Yet precisely because the separation has entered their minds, they cannot find the Infinite within themselves. They cannot open the flow of wisdom and energy from the Infinite through themselves. Therefore, they cannot fulfill their intended role of having dominion over the Earth and co-creating – by allowing the Infinite to work hitherto as they work – the abundant life on Earth. They have allowed the dualistic mind to have dominion over them.

As the illusion of separation densifies, many people fall into the one extreme of waiting for an external savior to come and save them. Others go into the opposite extreme of denying the existence of the Infinite and anything outside their self-created mental box.

Very few see the reality that no external savior will come because the Infinite respects its own laws, including the law of free will. The inhabitants of Earth have been given dominion over the Earth, meaning they can do with it as they please. If they want to turn it into a planet with lack and suffering, they have the right to do so, and no being who is one with the Infinite is allowed to interfere.

Conditions can change only when a critical mass of people begin to awaken from the illusion of separation and shake off the dualistic lies. Thereby, they can return to their true identity as co-creators with the Infinite, and they can now use their creative faculties to send a different impulse into the cosmic mirror. The mirror will gladly comply and will thus reflect back material circumstances that provide the abundant life for all.

Practitioners of non-war accept who they are and why they are here. They know that with "men" – with any finite means – it is impossible to overcome the current lack and suffering on Earth. Yet with the Infinite – working through themselves – all things are indeed possible.

***

Once a planet has descended into the illusion of separation, how can the situation be changed, how can the death spiral be broken? If the collective illusion has become so strong that it overpowers the individual minds of all inhabitants, how can anyone overcome this illusion on an individual basis? How can individuals come together to form a critical mass that can shift the collective consciousness? How can the downward spiral be turned around, once it has passed the point of no return?

The time-honored way is that beings from the spiritual realm volunteer to descend to a planet in order to demonstrate that any inhabitant has the potential to rise above duality and become an open door for the power, wisdom and love of the Infinite. Many such spiritual examples have been sent to Earth, some have been recognized and some have not.

The forces of war naturally do not want such teachers to be successful in awakening the people to the fact that everyone has the potential to overcome duality and unite with the Infinite. They want the people to remain trapped in duality, so they will keep feeding their energies to the forces of war, the energies that keep those forces alive.

The forces of war will seek to prevent the people from recognizing a non-dualistic teacher when he or she appears on Earth. If a teacher becomes recognized, the forces of war will attempt to silence or even kill the teacher in order to destroy the teaching. If killing the teacher does not stop the spread of the teaching, they will attempt to destroy the teaching. This is most easily done by elevating the teacher to an exception, in order to make the people believe that they cannot follow the example of the teacher and manifest the state of consciousness demonstrated by the teacher.

The lie is that the teacher was someone special and thus only the teacher could be an open door for the Infinite. This was possible only because the teacher came from the Infinite. And since all other people do not, they cannot possibly unite with the Infinite.

The reality is that all self-aware beings have a spark of the Infinite's Being and have the potential to serve as co-creators with the Infinite. The teacher comes to demonstrate a way that all can follow, which is why all true teachers say, "The works that I do, ye shall do also." The teacher is not fundamentally different from all other people but is merely further along on the path of union with the Infinite — the path that is open to all.

In past ages, the forces of war have been quite successful in destroying the examples of the teachers that were sent to set the people free from their self-denial, the denial of themselves as extensions of the Infinite. Thus, the members of the force of peace have determined to take a different approach in this age.

In this age many teachers have been sent at the same time. For when millions of people rise to claim their oneness with the Infinite, how can one be elevated to an idol? By seeing many people openly following the way beyond duality, many more people can be awakened and acknowledge their potential to follow the universal way.

The greatest need on Earth in this age is for the ones sent to awaken and acknowledge who they are and why they are here. They must be awakened and claim their oneness with the Infinite and then their oneness with each other. Only this will bring about the planetary awakening that is the highest potential for Earth in this age.

***

Practitioners of non-war recognize that the population of Earth can be divided into three groups, based on their level of consciousness:

- The top ten percent are the most spiritually aware people. They have escaped the blindness of selfishness and are willing to work for the greater vision of the Infinite, the cause of awakening all people to the abundant life. These people are close to seeing through the dualistic illusions, but because they were not brought up with an understanding of the dualistic mind, they might need an outer teaching in order to be awakened. They often have no outer characteristics that set them apart, for their attainment is an inner attainment that empowers them to recognize the reality of the Infinite and thus see beyond the dualistic illusions.

- The eighty percent of the general population. These are beings who cannot yet recognize the Infinite of their own accord. They need examples to follow, for they are partly blinded by the illusions of duality.

- The lowest ten percent of the most self-centered people. These are the people who are completely blinded by duality. They have often attained some mastery of the material realm – including how to attain power and wealth through the use of force – and hold prominent positions in society. In their spiritual blindness, they often think they are in a separate category that makes them better than the people. They often believe they are the saviors of the people or that they have some superior right to rule the Earth. They form a power elite who are seeking to make the people follow them, and they are willing to use ignorance or force to control the people. They do not understand that the Infinite is no respecter of persons.

The deciding factor for the future of the Earth is whether the people continue to follow the lowest ten percent – the blind leaders of the power elite – or whether they will start following the top ten percent, the enlightened leaders.

For this to happen, the top ten percent must awaken and dare to serve as examples. Can the spiritual "elite" step up and demonstrate the universal path with such clarity that the people will see it and start following them instead of the blind leaders of the power elite?

In pursuing this goal, it is essential for the spiritual elite to avoid falling into the trap of feeling superior to the people or to the power elite. They must remain meek, for only then will they inherit the Earth.

It is essential that the top ten percent all become practitioners of the art of non-war. For only by understanding the nature of the dualistic mind, can they resist the temptation to be pulled into a dualistic struggle against the power elite.

***

Some people are unaware of or deny that there is a struggle between good and evil, often even denying that there is evil in the world. Some people recognize evil and think the Earth is engulfed in an epic struggle between good and evil, often seen as a struggle between God and the devil.

None of these people have understood the reality of the struggle. They do not see that while there *is* a struggle on Earth, the struggle is not ultimately real. The reason is that none of the forces locked in the struggle are ultimately real. Neither good nor evil – as defined by most people – is ultimately real.

The Infinite is One. It is indivisible, it is everywhere present. There can be no divisions in the Infinite. If there can be no divisions, there can be no separation. If there can be no separation, there can be no split into two sides that oppose each other. And if there can be no opposing sides, there can be no struggle.

In the undivided reality of the Infinite, there can be no epic struggle between good and evil. For the Infinite could not possibly be in opposition to itself.

The struggle between good and evil has only a temporary existence. It can exist only in the minds of self-aware beings who have used their free will to accept the illusion of separation. They have used their creative faculties to form mental images of separation and send them into the cosmic mirror. This has forced the mirror to reflect back material circumstances that make separation seem real. Yet the struggle between opposing forces can continue only as long as a critical mass of self-aware beings choose to reinforce the source of the struggle, namely the dualistic mind.

The illusion of separation is what makes it possible that there can be opposing sides. In the Infinite, there can be no opposing sides. Opposing sides are born out of the illusion of separation.

***

The most subtle aspect of the illusion of separation is that it makes it seem like it is possible to be in opposition to the Infinite. Many self-aware beings have become blinded by the ultimate illusion, namely that there is a force that is in opposition to the Infinite and could even become stronger – at least on Earth – than the Infinite.

Many of the members of the forces of war are firmly convinced that they are in opposition to the Infinite and can force the Infinite to give them the world as a separate kingdom. The ultimate dualistic illusion is that the devil is actually in opposition to God.

Nothing can be in opposition to the true God of the Infinite. Thus, the stark reality is that the devil – the dualistic mind – can never be in opposition to the true God of the Infinite. The devil can be in opposition only to a false god that is created out of the illusion of separation.

What most people see as good and evil both spring from the illusion of separation. Therefore, taking one side in the battle between relative good and relative evil will only serve to perpetuate the dualistic struggle between these two finite – and illusory – forces.

The most subtle illusion of all is that the mind that has created the illusion of separation is in opposition to the Infinite. Yet the mind that is one with the Infinite knows that the Infinite cannot be divided. Thus, this mind also sees that the separate mind is *not* in opposition to the Infinite.

The reason is that the separate mind is not one mind. From its birth, the separate mind is divided into two. For only in the division into two can it separate out from the indivisible oneness of the Infinite. Thus, the separate mind is born not as one separate mind but as two separate minds.

These two minds must – in order to remain separate from the oneness of the Infinite – be separate from each other, meaning that they can only be in opposition to each other. It is the very creation of these two minds that gives rise to the illusion that there can be opposition.

Precisely because the separate minds cannot see their own unreality – for if they could, they would no longer be separate from the indivisible oneness of the Infinite – they cannot see that both polarities spring from the same basic illusion. Thus, each of the separate minds believes it is real and in alignment with ultimate reality while the other mind is unreal.

Some of those who are blinded by duality believe they form a force that is in opposition to God and can even become more powerful than God. Others who are blinded by duality believe they form a force that is in alignment with God and is doing God's work by fighting the force that opposes God. These are the forces that are locked in the "epic" struggle between so-called "good" and so-called "evil."

Practitioners of non-war, having opened their minds to the non-dualistic wisdom of the Infinite, understand how the one illusion of separation must give birth to the two opposing forces of duality. Thus, they know that both of these forces are relative, meaning that they can exist *only* in relation to each other. One cannot exist without the other, thus none of the two forces can be one with or in opposition to the Infinite.

Practitioners of non-war see that the epic struggle between good and evil is *not* a struggle between the Infinite and the devil. It is a struggle between two relative forces – relative good and relative evil – that both spring from the illusion of separation. It is a struggle between a finite god and a finite devil, both springing from the mind of duality.

The force of peace is not in opposition to the forces of war. It does not seek to destroy evil but to awaken people from the dualistic illusions. These illusions prevent people from seeing that it is the forces of war that have split into those representing relative good and those representing relative evil. Thus, the forces of war are not fighting the force of peace, for how can you fight someone who is not fighting back? The forces of war are fighting amongst themselves. They are warring within their own members.

Practitioners of non-war see that the forces of war are – without fully understanding why – seeking to perpetuate this struggle indefinitely. Thus, practitioners of non-war know that taking either side in this struggle will not enhance the non-dualistic cause of the Infinite. It will only serve to reinforce the dualistic struggle that keeps people separated from the Infinite.

Practitioners of non-war see that, throughout history, countless people have been lured into taking part in the relative, dualistic struggle. They came to believe in the dualistic illusion that they were fighting for some ultimate good, even killing others in the name of God. Thus, practitioners of non-war make it their goal to stay out of this dualistic struggle and to awaken others to the folly of thinking that relative good can ever eradicate relative evil.

Practitioners of non-war understand that the power elite – the forces of war – do not want the dualistic struggle to end. They want it to continue indefinitely, because it is the only way for them to survive. Only as long as people engage in the struggle, will they give their energies to the forces of war. Only as long as the struggle continues, will a small elite be able to take power and wealth away from the people Only through the struggle can the elite maintain the resistance that keeps them from flowing with the River of Life.

***

Practitioners of non-war see that the struggle started because certain self-aware beings became infatuated with the concept of separation. In the oneness of the Infinite, no self-aware being can be better or more important than another, for there are no comparisons in infinity. Yet once separation has occurred, self-aware beings can be divided into groups, some forming the leaders and some the followers, some being superior and some inferior.

Separation leads to division and division makes comparisons possible. Yet division also gives birth to lack and loss, causing some to have more and some to have less, some to be the "haves" and some to be the "have-nots." Only when there is inequality is there a basis for comparison.

This division into high and low is what has allowed a small group of self-aware beings to form a power elite that has controlled the people in all societies seen in recorded history. The members of this elite have caused or instigated all of the wars an atrocities known to human-kind.

Why have the people failed to see this? Why haven't they stopped giving their energy to the power elite, thereby inevitably causing this elite to shrink into insignificance? Because too many people are content to be blind followers, whereby they can avoid taking responsibility for themselves.

Practitioners of non-war see that the forces of war are led by the power elite but that many among the people are unknowingly supporting the dualistic struggle. They do so because they do not want to take responsibility for themselves but want others to make decisions for them. This has created an unholy alliance between those who want to be superior – by having power over others – and those who do not want to make decisions, thus being willing to give away their power.

Practitioners of non-war know that status quo will change only when a sufficient number of people see through this state of consciousness and decide to align themselves with the reality of the Infinite. This planet cannot be set free from the dualistic struggle by destroying the forces of war.

The planet will be free only when the collective consciousness is raised, so that people can begin to see through the illusions of war. The key to lasting peace is *not* to destroy the forces of war but to make them irrelevant by neutralizing their dualistic lies with the non-dualistic wisdom of the Infinite.

***

Practitioners of non-war know that evil has no ultimate reality, and thus it is futile to spend one's life seeking to destroy that which is unreal. Far better to replace the unreality by dedicating one's life to bringing the incomparable reality of the Infinite into every situation.

Since relative good can never exist without relative evil – and vice versa – how could one force possibly eradicate the other? Those who think this is possible are simply trapped in the endless struggle that will never bring peace on Earth, good will among people.

Practitioners of non-war see that even those who claim to be fighting for God's cause have created a false god based on a graven image. Thus, practitioners of non-war reach beyond all graven images, until they have a direct inner experience of the non-dualistic reality of the Infinite.

Practitioners of non-war follow the admonishment of all true spiritual teachers, namely to go out into the world and preach a non-dualistic gospel to all creatures, turning all people into followers of the true, non-dualistic teachers of humankind. Only when there is oneness between the self-aware beings in Spirit and the self-aware beings on Earth, will the sacred figure-eight flow manifest the Golden Age of the Infinite on Earth.

Made in the USA